THE MEDITATOR'S WORKBOOK

THE MEDITATOR'S WORKBOOK
A Journey to the Center

Matthew Flickstein

Foreword by Bhante Gunaratana

Wisdom Publications • Boston

Wisdom Publications
199 Elm Street
Somerville MA 02144 USA
www.wisdompubs.org

Library of Congress Cataloging-in-Publication Data
Flickstein, Matthew.
 The meditator's workbook : a journey to the center / Matthew Flickstein.
   p. cm.
 Previously published under title: Journey to the Center.
 Includes index.
 ISBN 0-86171-586-1 (pbk. : alk. paper)
 1. Self-actualization (Psychology) 2. Meditation. I. Flickstein, Matthew. Journey to the Center. II. Title.
 BF637.S4F58 2009
 158.1'2—dc22
                                    2009006817

13 12 11 10 09
5 4 3 2 1

Cover image by Gopa&Ted2.
Cover design by Tony Lulek with thanks to Jim Zaccaria.
Interior design by TLLC. Set in Weiss 12/16.
Oxherding woodblock prints by Tomikichiro Tokuriki.
Illustrations of meditators by Loel Barr.

Wisdom Publications' books are printed on acid-free paper and meet the guidelines for permanence and durability of the Production Guidelines for Book Longevity of the Council on Library Resources.

Printed in the United States of America.

This book was produced with environmental mindfulness. We have elected to print this title on 30% PCW recycled paper. As a result, we have saved the following resources: 13 trees, 9 million BTUs of energy, 1,121 lbs. of greenhouse gases, 4,632 gallons of water, and 560 lbs. of solid waste. For more information, please visit our website, www.wisdompubs.org. This paper is also FSC certified. For more information, please visit www.fscus.org.

CONTENTS

TO CAROL, MY DEVOTED WIFE,
FRIEND, TEACHER, AND SPIRITUAL PARTNER.

This is not another book you read passively—as if reading a novel curled up in a chair. This book invites you to put what you read into action. It is the kind of book that can change your life and point you to greater peace and happiness.

I have known Matthew Flickstein for more than twenty years. His way of teaching Dhamma and psychology is unique, because he knows how to bridge the two, blending them together so perfectly that his students can benefit from both. Through stories and illustrations Matthew drives his points home.

Meditation and psychology are often seen as mere theories. For this author, they are much more. He has made both subjects so lively that even an uninterested reader will want to take a second look.

Some people say Buddhism is a psychology; others say it is a philosophy. Some say it is a religion; others say it is a way of life. Matthew has integrated all of these approaches and does so with magnificent clarity.

When most people read books that are practical in nature, they rarely follow through on the instructions or advice. Generally, they don't bother to read with a note pad at hand. When they do take the time to write down important points, they may forget about them or fail to put them into practice. Matthew has made all of this easy for his readers by providing exercise pages with room to write. Matthew is a practical man, and so is his book. Exercises and journal entries, in addition to using traditional teaching methods, help readers become more deeply involved in Dhamma practice. It is not easy to teach Dhamma so that people practice it as we teach it, but Matthew uses a most effective method. He inspires your imagination, emotions, and intellectual participation while making the "journey to the center."

Bhante Gunaratana

ACKNOWLEDGMENTS

I am fortunate to have met Bhante Gunaratana, who has been a guiding light and a constant source of inspiration over the years. Other teachers who have profoundly influenced the direction of my life and the writing of this book include Bhikkhu Bodhi, Eido Tai Shimano-roshi, and Stanley Krippner.

My wife, Carol, has been an unwavering source of support and has spent untold hours editing the manuscript. My children, Richard and Debra, have offered invaluable feedback. I am grateful for the suggestions offered by Walter Schwidetzky, Lynne Drabkin, and Bill Mueller. I appreciate the efforts of Laura Neidlinger, who typed the manuscript, of Peter Slavin who helped with the editing process, and of the entire staff of Wisdom Publications. Finally, this work could not have been completed without the loving support of friends such as Elizabeth Loo-Vinnedge, Tom Quinn, and Bruce Mitteldorf.

Every individual I have encountered has been either a guide or a traveling companion on my inner journey. This book is an expression of appreciation for their contributions to my life.

INTRODUCTION

What would it be like if you had always been the only person in the world? Would you know if you were a man or a woman, whether you were rich or poor, caring or insensitive? If there had never been anyone else but you, none of these categories would exist.

If we reflect deeply, we will discover that every way we have defined ourselves has always been in relation to something or someone else. If this is true, who are we beyond our self-definitions?

The "journey to the center" is the quest to answer this question for ourselves. The goal of this journey is to move beyond the externals in order to reach the very essence of our lives. It is to become authentic and to realize and express our true vision in the world. It is to come home to a place of unconditional love, inner peace, and clarity of mind.

Our work together will be intense, the views along the way will be extraordinary, and the overall experience will be transformative. I am delighted that you have chosen to join this expedition.

Before we take to the road, there are certain preparations to be made in order to insure that we will arrive safely at our destination. These include: understanding the goal of our journey, examining the map we will be following, and learning a technique that will enable us to effectively navigate the obstacles we are bound to encounter along the way.

THE GOAL OF THE JOURNEY

There are two characteristics of the human mind that are essential to recognize if we are to fully understand the goal of our journey. The first characteristic is that virtually everyone's mind—to some degree—is confused.

If we describe mental health in terms of a continuum, at one extreme are individuals whom we refer to as "psychotic." These are people who have lost touch with consensual reality and live in a world of their own. At the other end of the continuum are individuals whom we refer to as "enlightened" (figure 1).

Psychotic   Enlightened

FIGURE 1

Fully enlightened beings have perfect mental health and experience a profound sense of well-being. They have resolved all the issues from their past, have no fears regarding the future, and are able to live fully in the present moment. Their minds are no longer riddled with doubts, troubled by obsessions, or motivated by hatred and greed. They are loving, compassionate, and exhibit an infinite amount of patience in the face of adversity.

You may have noticed the break in the continuum shown in figure 1. This break, prior to the point of enlightenment, illustrates that enlightenment requires a synaptic jump (rather than a gradual unfolding) to a transcendent level of awareness. The jump represents a shift from dealing with the content of the mind to being able to see the mind as a conditioned process. This phenomenon will be explained in greater detail later.

The distribution of mental health is similar to a bell-shaped curve, with the middle and greatest portion representing what society considers "normal" (figure 2). Although we may be quite normal, the degree to which we have not achieved full enlightenment is the degree to which confusion is still present in our minds.

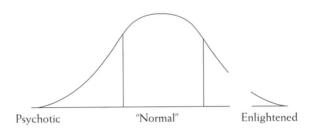

| Psychotic | "Normal" | Enlightened |

FIGURE 2

A second characteristic of the human mind is that we have an innate drive to keep moving toward the enlightenment end of the mental health continuum. Most of us, however, do not acknowledge or even realize that we are striving to become enlightened. This inward pull is usually described as the quest to achieve greater happiness, contentment, psychological freedom, or meaning in one's life.

Taking these two mental characteristics into account (that virtually everyone's mind is confused to some degree and that we are naturally inclined to keep moving toward enlightenment), the specific goal of our journey is to reach the center of our being, the source of the enlightenment we seek.

STAGES OF THE JOURNEY

The journey you will follow and the sights you will see as you move closer to your destination are represented by the Ten Oxherding Pictures. The ox symbolizes your true nature, the reality that lies beyond your conditioned and transitory existence. "Herding the wild ox" is a metaphor for the progressive stages of realization that you will encounter during your quest for enlightenment.

A Chinese Zen master conceived of the stages illustrated in these pictures during the Sung dynasty in the twelfth century A.D. He based his model upon an earlier Taoist version which had eight pictures and ended with the empty circle entitled "Both Ox and Self Transcended." The last two stages were added to describe the experience of living at the center of our being and to demonstrate the importance of applying this inner understanding to our daily life. The following is a brief description of what you can expect to encounter during each stage of the journey:

 Searching for the Ox. You recognize that what you are truly seeking is contentment, not just happiness—inner peace rather than outward excitement.

 Discovering the Footprints. You realize that the journey to the center takes place within your own mind.

 Perceiving the Ox. You uncover the ways in which you have unconsciously defined yourself, and you realize how profoundly these self-images have affected the quality of your life.

Catching the Ox. You begin to resolve your issues from the past and start to confront your fears regarding the future.

 Taming the Ox. You learn how to maintain a moment-to-moment awareness of the thoughts that incessantly arise within your mind.

 Riding the Ox Home. You learn to live in the moment, in the "here and now" of your life.

 The Ox Transcended. You unify your fragmented mind as you begin to live in harmony with the natural rhythm of your life.

 Both Ox and Self Transcended. You realize who you are beyond your self-definitions.

 Reaching the Source. You reach the center of your being, and your psychological and spiritual struggles finally come to an end.

 In the World. You learn to integrate your new understanding with the rest of your life and to appreciate the joy of sharing with others what you have come to understand.

The "Ten Oxherding Pictures" is only a model that illustrates the path to enlightenment. The stages are not mutually exclusive, where one step must be completed before the next one can be taken. You may find yourself working on several stages simultaneously.

During each stage of your journey you will be challenged by three tasks. The first task is to gain a conceptual understanding of the insights associated with the stage at which you are currently working. The second is to acknowledge and examine the obstacles that have to be surmounted for those insights to be realized. The final task is to engage in a series of exercises designed to eliminate the obstacles that block these insights.

NAVIGATING OBSTACLES

When planning an expedition, we have to consider the possibility of meeting with problems that will require the use of special skills. On this journey there is one danger, difficulty, or obstacle that almost everyone encounters. This obstacle, which could prevent us from reaching our goal, is the tendency to become lost in the drama of our minds.

The nature of this obstacle is similar to snow blindness, where, due to constant exposure to ultraviolet rays, we lose the ability to see clearly what may be right in front of our eyes. Getting stuck in the drama of our minds is a kind of psychic blindness. It is caused, in part, by the constant exposure of our minds to the conditioned ways of thinking reflected by most people in the world. If we identify with these conditioned ways of thinking and believe that they are true, we unconsciously grasp at them whenever they enter our minds. When we suffer from psychic blindness, we lose the ability to see the bare truth, which lies just beyond our own points of view.

The best way of dealing with snow blindness is to prevent it. We can wear protective goggles to eliminate, or at least reduce, the amount of ultraviolet light to which we are exposed. Similarly, the most effective way of handling psychic blindness is to prevent it. We can use a technique that is designed to keep us centered in the awareness of each new moment, enabling us to eliminate, or at least reduce, the amount of psychic distortion to which we are exposed. The following analogy illustrates the nature of this technique.

If we want to tame four animals (an elephant, an eagle, an alligator, and an ape), and we attempt to do so by tying them all together with one piece of rope (figure 3), we will not be very successful! Each animal will try to pull the others into its own domain. The ape would try to drag the other animals into the trees, the eagle would try to lift them into the air, the elephant would try to force them into the jungle, and the alligator would attempt to pull them into the water.

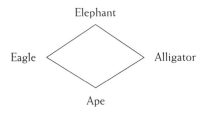

FIGURE 3

However, if we were to drive a post securely into the ground and tie each animal to that post individually (figure 4), should the animals try to escape, they would quickly discover that they were unable to do so. After struggling for a while, they would come to rest quietly by the side of the post.

These animals signify the content of our minds. The elephant stands for our memories, the alligator symbolizes our feelings, the ape represents our recurring concerns, and the eagle stands for our goals and aspirations. It is as though our thoughts and feelings are all tied together with one piece of rope. When a thought or feeling that we consider to be significant enters our mind, it tends to pull the rest of our mind in its direction. Memories of the past may drag along feelings of guilt, money considerations may bring with them feelings of fear, and so forth.

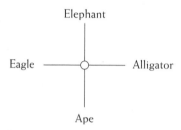

FIGURE 4

We are controlled only by those mental processes of which we are unaware. If we create a "post of awareness" in the mind and tie our thoughts and feelings to that post as they enter our minds, when those thoughts and feelings try to take control they will quickly discover that they are unable to do so. After struggling for a while, they will come to rest quietly by the side of this post.

This post of awareness, which eventually eliminates the conditioned reactivity of the mind, can be cultivated through the practice of insight meditation. Since we need to avoid becoming lost in the drama of our minds from the very beginning of our journey, we will start by reviewing the instructions on how to practice this form of meditation.

You can meditate one or more times per day, but attempt to be consistent in your practice. Most experienced meditators "sit" for either forty-five or sixty minutes. You can start with twenty minutes and gradually increase the amount of time you spend in each session.

To practice insight meditation, sit on either a hard cushion placed on top of a mat or on a straight-back chair. If you choose to sit on the floor, you can assume any one of four postures (the full lotus, the half lotus, the quarter lotus, or the uncrossed position).

In the full lotus (figure 5), the right foot is placed over the left thigh, and the left foot is placed over the right thigh, with both knees touching the mat for support. For all of the floor positions, it is helpful to sit on the first third of the cushion (figure 6). This makes it easier for your knees to touch the mat, which creates a more stable posture. The spine is erect and the knees are in line with one another. The full lotus is typically a very difficult posture for new meditators to assume.

In the half lotus (figure 7), either the right foot is placed over the left thigh, or the left foot is placed over the right thigh, with both knees touching the mat. In the quarter lotus

FIGURE 5   FIGURE 6   FIGURE 7

(figure 8), either the right foot is resting on the left calf, or the left foot is resting on the right calf. In either position it may be necessary to place a small cushion under the knee furthest from the floor for support until your body adjusts.

In the uncrossed position (figure 9), either the left or the right foot is in front, with both legs and knees touching the mat. If you choose to sit on a straight-back chair (figure 10), you can insert a flat cushion between your back and the rear of the chair. Your feet should be placed firmly on the ground.

In all cases, your posture is straight but relaxed. Your left hand is palm up and placed in your lap with your right hand, also palm up, on top of the left. (The reverse of this hand position is also acceptable.)

Make a commitment to remain still during the entire meditation period. The reason for this commitment is illustrated by the analogy of the magnifying glass. If you want to use a magnifying glass to focus the sun's rays so that they burn through a piece of paper, you need to hold the magnifying glass steady, avoiding any unnecessary movements of the hand. If you keep moving the glass around, you will not focus the sun's rays, and, as a result, you will not generate the heat needed to burn through the paper.

FIGURE 8   FIGURE 9   FIGURE 10

Similarly, if you want to focus your attention in order to penetrate the reality of your moment-to-moment experience, you need to keep your mind steady and free from unnecessary distractions. Your mind becomes disturbed every time you move your body. When your mind is disturbed, you are unable to generate the amount of concentration required to see through your mental conditioning.

The instructions on how to practice insight meditation have been divided into four parts. The first part teaches you how to calm your mind (page 12), the second how to work with sensory distractions that may arise (chapter four), the third how to develop an awareness of your mental and emotional habits (chapter five), and the fourth how to reach deeper levels of awareness (chapter nine).

It may be helpful to record the following instructions and play them back during your first few meditation sessions. *Leave enough time after each statement so that you can practice what you are being instructed to do.* You can record the sound of a bell at the end of forty-five or sixty minutes to signal the end of the session.

INSIGHT MEDITATION INSTRUCTIONS

CALMING THE MIND

❖ Your eyes are closed.

❖ Your mouth is closed and you are breathing through your nose.

❖ Feel the sensation of your breath as it flows in and out of your nostrils at the tip of your nose. Some people feel the sensation more strongly within the nostrils, while others feel it more on the upper lip.

❖ To help you locate where you feel the touch sensation of the breath most distinctly, inhale deeply and force the air out through your nostrils. Wherever you feel the sensation most clearly and precisely is the place to focus your attention for the balance of the meditation period.

❖ Feel the beginning, the middle, and the end of every in-breath, and the beginning, the middle, and the end of every out-breath.

❖ Sometimes the breath will be short—there is no need to make it longer. Sometimes the breath will be long—there is no need to make it shorter. Sometimes the breath will be erratic—there is no need to even it out.

❖ Just become aware of the breath as it goes in and
    out of the nostrils at the tip of the nose.

❖ Feel the beginning, the middle, and the end of
    every in-breath, and the beginning, the middle,
    and the end of every out-breath.

❖ Let the breath breathe itself.

❖ Every time your attention moves away from the
    breath and shifts to a different object of
    awareness, such as a physical sensation or a
    thought, gently but firmly draw your attention
    back to the touch sensation of your breath.

❖ Continue practicing until the end of the medita-
    tion session.

How do you feel right now? Did you find yourself calming
down as you focused on the breath? The reason we typically do
not feel calm is that the mind is usually scattered in many directions. As we focus on a single object (like the breath), the mind
tends to calm down on its own.

A certain degree of concentration or calm is essential for
the successful practice of meditation, but that is not the ultimate goal. We are actually trying to develop insight into the
nature of our experience. The way we accomplish this will
become more apparent when we review the next set of instructions. Until that time, continue to work on calming your mind.

CHAPTER ONE

SEARCHING FOR THE OX

INSIGHTS: HAPPINESS VERSUS INNER PEACE

Throughout our lives we have been searching for a lasting sense of happiness. Happiness refers to a state of mind, however, that is always dependent upon circumstances. When our circumstances match our aspirations we feel happy, and when they do not, we feel unhappy. Therefore, our search has always fallen short of its mark. We may have experienced many moments of happiness, but we have never been able to string those moments together to create a continuous experience of happiness. The reason for this is that life is by nature problematic; it never totally conforms to what our ego believes will make it happy. The problems and issues that we deal with from day to day may change form, but they will never disappear.

Contentment, unlike happiness, is not dependent upon our circumstances. It is an inner perspective from which we are aware of the difficulties or problems of our lives without being emotionally controlled by them. Contentment is an experience of inner peace. It is like being in the eye of a hurricane; the hurricane of our lives may still be swirling around us, but we are no longer caught up in the turmoil.

The journey to the center begins with the insight that, while there is nothing intrinsically wrong with pursuing happiness, it does not bring lasting satisfaction. True satisfaction comes instead from contentment or peace of mind.

OBSTACLES: GRATIFICATION AND RESISTANCE

What prevents us from recognizing that life is inherently problematic and that we can never experience a lasting sense of happiness? It is the immediate and powerful gratification that occurs when we encounter experiences pleasing to our senses. This instant satisfaction keeps us looking for the "ultimate carrot," which always seems to lie just beyond our reach.

Another obstacle to acknowledging the troublesome nature of life is an inner emotional resistance. This stems from the fear that, if we acknowledged that life was by nature problematic, we might be depressed all of the time, feeling helpless to do anything about it. Learning to be content in the face of adversity requires the intentional cultivation of specific mental qualities. Few individuals are even aware of what these qualities are, and fewer still know how to intentionally cultivate them.

PATH: REVIEWING OUR LIVES

Our first exercise will enable you to create a visual representation of what your life has been like over the years. The purpose of this exercise is to demonstrate the problematic nature of your own path through life.

EXERCISE: TRACING A PATH THROUGH LIFE

❖ Use a clean sheet of unlined paper or the space provided in this book.

❖ Place your pen or pencil on the left hand edge of the paper, halfway down from the top. This point symbolizes the day you were born.

❖ Draw a graphic representation of your life indicating the ups and downs you experienced from the day you were born until this moment in time.

❖ Although in retrospect you may be able to see the good that came out of each of your difficult or painful experiences, for this exercise illustrate what each experience felt like at the time you went through it.

The following example is one person's drawing:

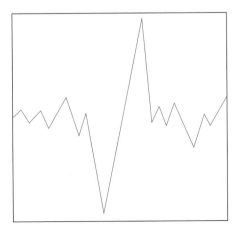

MY PATH THROUGH LIFE

Did your drawing indicate that there have been ups and downs throughout your life? Join the club! Everyone belongs.

Some individuals create drawings where their final lines are pointing downward. This typically signifies that the people who drew them are currently dealing with an issue in their lives. On the other hand, when the drawings end with the final lines pointing upward, it usually indicates that the people who drew them currently feel positive about the direction their lives are going. In what direction does your final line point? What does that indicate to you?

We never seem to have enough of what we want in our lives. We want to stay young, but we become old. We want to remain healthy, but we fall ill. We want our loving relationships to endure, but circumstances and feelings change. We spend many years cultivating our careers, but we are replaced by the next generation. We want our money to last, but unexpected expenses keep arising. We look forward to retirement, but we may be too old or ill to enjoy it.

The result of trying to get a lasting sense of happiness from an impermanent set of circumstances is stress. There are two kinds of stress; eustress and distress. Eustress is a positive kind of stress that motivates us to achieve our goals. Distress is debilitating and impairs our ability to produce satisfactory results in our life.

In the next exercise you will evaluate just how much distress you have been experiencing and the ways in which it may be manifesting itself within your life.

EXERCISE: IDENTIFYING SYMPTOMS OF STRESS

Please indicate which symptoms you experience from time to time and how often you experience them:

PHYSICAL SYMPTOMS	YES	NO	FREQUENCY
Headaches			
Backaches			
Stomach aches			
Neck aches			
Heart palpitations			
High blood pressure			
Sweaty palms			
Dry mouth			
Hives			
Sleepiness during the day			

SYMPTOMS AT WORK	YES	NO	FREQUENCY
Feeling uncomfortable around management			
Trying not to be noticed			
Losing perspective and getting stuck on details			
Hating to be disturbed when busy			
Consistent dissatisfaction with your results			
Feeling that there is never enough time			
Thinking that too many things are happening at once			
Experiencing excessive internal pressure to perform			

PSYCHOLOGICAL SYMPTOMS	YES	NO	FREQUENCY
Overeating or consistently eating a lot of sweets			
Mood swings or recurring depressions			
A lack of energy or ambition			
Indecisiveness or confusion			
Impatience			
Guilt feelings			
Problems falling asleep, tossing and turning during the night, or problems getting out of bed in the morning			
Worrying about things that may never take place			
Difficulty dealing with change			
Fear of criticism or rejection			
Fear of losing someone's love			
Imagining the worst possible things happening to you			

Reflecting on the amount of distress we experience may generate some unpleasant feelings. However, they are warning signs that all is not well with our lives. Whether the symptoms are manifesting physically or psychologically, they should not be ignored. Aside from the possibility of leading to illness, they are providing us with a message about the problematic nature of life. Unless the insight into the difficulties inherent in life is internalized, we will continue our futile search for a lasting sense of happiness. We will also lack the motivation to sustain the energy necessary to complete the journey. When we begin to focus primarily on seeking contentment or inner peace, our search for the ox has truly begun.

CHAPTER TWO

DISCOVERING THE FOOTPRINTS

INSIGHTS: TRUE POWER COMES FROM WITHIN

There was once a stonecutter who earned his living chipping small rocks from enormous boulders. For twenty-five years, he toiled and his hands became as hard as the boulders upon which he worked. One day, as he began chipping at a new boulder, it cracked open and a magic lamp fell to the ground. When the stonecutter picked up the lamp and rubbed it, a genie appeared and in a booming voice said to him, "I will grant you all of the wishes that you believe will increase your power in life."

After some thought the stonecutter replied, "If I had enough money that I could just lie on my couch, gaze out of the window, and watch the world go by, that would give me the sense of power I am after." In the very next moment, the stonecutter found himself lying on his couch with piles of money next to him.

As the stonecutter looked out his window, he noticed a king being carried along on a raised platform as his many attendants fanned him. "There's no power in just lying here on my couch," thought the stonecutter. "True power comes from being a king." As he uttered these words, the stonecutter was immediately transformed into the king and found himself being carried along on that very same platform.

He soon realized, however, why the attendants were fanning him: It was so hot that no matter how hard they fanned, he still felt the sun burning his skin. "There's no real power in being a king," thought the stonecutter. "True power comes from being the sun." In the next moment, the king became the sun.

As the sun, he heated all the regions of the world and brought the light of day to the earth. But quite unexpectedly, a rain cloud floated beneath him and prevented him from shining where he chose to direct his rays. "There is no power in being the sun," realized the stonecutter. "True power comes from being a rain cloud." Quicker than a sudden burst of rain, the sun became that rain cloud.

As the rain cloud, he flooded the valleys, filled up the oceans, and watered all the vegetation. However, he noticed that no matter how hard he tried to penetrate the huge rocks and boulders with his rain, he was unable to do so. "There is no power in being a rain cloud," thought the stonecutter. "True power comes from being one of those enormous boulders." In an instant, the cloud became one of the boulders that just a second before lay beneath him.

"Now," decided the stonecutter, "I have finally found true power!" And he thought that way for a while...until another stonecutter came along and started chipping at him, one piece at a time!

Most of us live with the question of how to gain mastery over our lives. We strive for financial stability, positions with responsibility, meaningful relationships, and even spiritual attainments as potential sources of personal power. Even when we achieve our aspirations, the experience somehow misses the mark. The insight we realize when we reach the stage of "discovering the ox's footprints" is that the power to achieve contentment or peace of mind comes from within and is not dependent upon the external circumstances of our lives.

Even when we realize the true source of self-mastery, the question of how to access it still remains. The following story illustrates how easy it is to miss the most obvious source of our inner wealth.

OBSTACLES: MISSING THE OBVIOUS

A very poor man lived near the border of two kingdoms. He slept in a grass hut, had only the clothing on his back, and appeared to own nothing but a donkey. Every day he would cross the border between the two kingdoms, taking his donkey along with him. At nightfall, he returned to his hut alone.

The border guards routinely checked to make sure that the man was not smuggling anything—though they had little concern since he was so poor. After several months of crossing the border, however, the man moved from his hut and wore new clothing each day. This did not go unnoticed by the border guards, who started checking more thoroughly as the man passed their post. They checked inside, over, and under the donkey's saddlebags, but found nothing except straw.

Eventually, the man who once owned nothing but a donkey became the richest person in the district. He moved into a palace and had many servants working for him.

Many years later, one of the border guards retired and came upon the wealthy merchant in the village square. "I have always wondered how you accumulated so much wealth," said the former border guard. "I was sure that you were smuggling something, but I could never discover what it was."

The merchant openly admitted that he had indeed been

smuggling something. "Since you no longer work for the government," said the man, "I will tell you what it was. You see, I was smuggling donkeys!"

Because the border guards were so focused on looking at the saddlebags, they missed the most obvious and important object of attention—the donkey itself! The theme of this story, that the obvious is often the most difficult to see, illustrates the type of obstacle that prevents us from realizing how to access the power that lies within. Most of us believe that it is our behavior that produces the results we seek in life:

BEHAVIORS———▶RESULTS

If we reflect on the content of our day-to-day thoughts, we discover that most of the time they are focused on what we have to do in order to obtain something we want. However, by focusing in this way, we miss the most obvious and most important object of attention: *how we think.*

It is not possible, as we will see shortly, to manifest any behavior without having it first begin as a thought in our mind. Our thinking process, not our behavior or our results, is the starting point of our journey. The main obstacle to "discovering the ox's footprints," therefore, is looking for them in the wrong places.

PATH: THE POWER OF IMAGES

Realizing for ourselves that the power to achieve contentment comes from within requires an understanding of how our thinking process controls our behaviors and thereby our results. Aside from reflex actions, each of our behaviors, whether physical, verbal, or psychological, is always preceded by an intention or a mental decision to express it. We may not always be aware of our intentions. Nevertheless, before we change our posture, utter a syllable, or decide on a course of action, intentions to perform these activities necessarily come first.

INTENTIONS———►BEHAVIORS———►RESULTS

Our intentions, in turn, are determined by and based upon our *self-image;* that is, who we think we are and what we believe we are capable of achieving. The thoughts which comprise our self-image thus dictate the scope and character of our intentions, behaviors, and results.

SELF-IMAGE———►INTENTIONS———►BEHAVIOR———►RESULTS

Although our self-image—the psychological perspective through which we see the world—plays such a crucial role in our lives, most of us are unaware of what it is. In the same way that the eye cannot see itself, we are blind to our own self-image. Because we are completely merged, or identified, with our self-image, we have no objective stance from which to view it.

Regardless of the results we consciously desire in our lives, our unconscious self-image will determine whether or not we will actually be able to produce them. This is because our self-image must be aligned with the results we are trying to achieve in order for us to manifest the appropriate intentions and behaviors. The following example will illustrate how this process operates.

When children are abused, they often make an unconscious judgment that the abuse is deserved. That judgment contributes to the development of a negative self-image. When these individuals eventually seek significant relationships, they consciously desire ones which are loving and supportive. Because of their negative self-images, however, they unconsciously gravitate to other abusive relationships.

If the abused individuals do form relationships with nurturing individuals, these relationships are usually short-lived. This occurs because of a psychological process called *cognitive dissonance.* Cognitive dissonance is the difference, incompatibility, or inconsistency between what we believe we deserve (i.e., our self-image) and what we are currently experiencing (i.e., our results). When this disparity occurs it creates psychological symptoms, such as anxiety and fear, or physical symptoms, such as headaches and nausea. We deal with these adverse reactions by (unconsciously) modifying our intentions and behaviors so that our results become compatible with our self-image, and the feeling of homeostasis or equilibrium is restored. This process occurs even though the results we obtain are contrary to those we consciously desire.

Our self-image can also be a positive influence in our lives. If our self-image is greater than our current set of circumstances, cognitive dissonance will motivate us to manifest the type of intentions and behaviors that will enable us to reach our desired objectives.

We actually have many "clusters" of self-images, each cluster corresponding to a different aspect of our lives. We think of ourselves differently depending upon which role we are playing at the moment (e.g., parent, student, friend). Some of these clusters may be healthy and helpful (e.g., believing that one is an effective parent), and others may be unhealthy and self-destructive (e.g., believing that one is not worthy of achieving prosperity). Whether healthy and helpful or unhealthy and self-destructive, our self-image and the process of cognitive dissonance affect our health, career, relationships, and overall sense of well-being every moment of our lives.

The following exercise should enable you to begin identifying some areas of your life in which your self-image may not be all that you would like it to be. We will revisit this exercise at a future point in the journey when we discuss the methods for transforming our self-image.

EXERCISE: RECOGNIZING UNACHIEVED GOALS

For each category, list the goals you have been consistently trying to achieve but have been unable to accomplish. Place a check next to those goals you have come close to reaching more than one time.

I HAVE COME CLOSE

1. Health related:

   a. _____

   b. _____

   c. _____

2. Financial:

   a. _____

   b. _____

   c. _____

3. Career:

    a. _____

    b. _____

    c. _____

4. Relationships:

    a. _____

    b. _____

    c. _____

5. Creative:

    a. _____

    b. _____

    c. _____

When we finally realize that our self-image is directly responsible for our intentions, behaviors, and results and that it could not be otherwise, we have "discovered the footprints" of the ox. Make sure to keep your eyes peeled: The ox may be just around the bend!

CHAPTER THREE

PERCEIVING THE OX

INSIGHTS: WE CAN REPROGRAM OUR MINDS

Once we have seen the footprints, we need to follow them until we actually "perceive" the ox. There are three insights that arise when we reach this level of awareness.

The first is the realization that, in order to recognize our self-image, we can no longer identify with it. In other words, we have to learn how to objectify our own mental processes. At this stage of the journey it is not our self-image that changes, but the way in which we relate to it. Our frame of reference shifts from one of identification to one of objective observation.

The second insight is that our current self-image is primarily cultivated through the unconscious programming of our minds. This programming has been directly influenced by the significant people in our lives and indirectly by the society in which we live.

The final insight is the understanding that we can create any self-image we choose by learning how to reprogram our minds. It does not matter how negative or self-limiting our current self-image is; it can become whatever we consciously wish it to be.

OBSTACLES: SELF-BLAME

Before we can change our self-image, we have to determine what it is right now. There are two psychological obstacles to making this determination. The first is that we believe we already know what our self-image is. As a consequence, when we are about to discover an aspect of our self-image which is contrary to who we think we are or what we believe we are capable of achieving, we suppress that feature in order to avoid experiencing the psychic conflict that would arise if we faced it.

The second obstacle is the tendency to blame ourselves for our current self-image. To avoid feelings of guilt that result from self-blame, we shy away from confronting our self-perceptions. Many of us have not made the distinction between responsibility and blame. As adults with mature mental faculties, we are clearly responsible for the content of our thoughts and images. Blame connotes judgment, however, and implies that we had total control over the programming of our minds that took place when we were young and impressionable and unable to filter the input we were receiving. If as a child, for example, you were constantly told that you were stupid, you may have formed a negative self-image regarding your intelligence. If you still maintain that self-image as an adult, you are responsible for its persistence. However, you are certainly not to blame for its origination.

PATH: UNCOVERING OUR SHADOW SELF

This phase of our journey consists of three parts. We begin by describing the relationship between the conscious, preconscious, and unconscious facets of the mind. This explanation is followed by an exercise designed to give you a direct experience of some of the thoughts, images, and feelings that lie just beyond your conscious awareness. Finally, we will discuss the ways in which our minds have become conditioned, and you will have an opportunity to start the process of intentionally reprogramming your mind.

THE CONSCIOUS, PRECONSCIOUS, AND UNCONSCIOUS

The metaphor of moving through a tunnel can be used to illustrate the relationship between the different aspects of the mind (figure 11) and the process by which we can reach deeper levels of self-understanding.

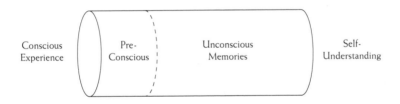

| Conscious Experience | Pre-Conscious | Unconscious Memories | Self-Understanding |

FIGURE 11   THE DIFFERENT FACETS OF THE MIND

Our conscious experience, or consciousness, is the moment-to-moment awareness of the sights, sounds, smells, tastes, and touch sensations that we experience through our five physical senses. It is also the moment-to-moment awareness of the feelings, perceptions, and other mental phenomena that we experience through our minds.

Just inside of the tunnel is the preconscious aspect of our minds. The preconscious is the repository of memories to which we have easy access. However, we typically avoid looking at those preconscious memories which call to mind the unresolved issues of our lives. These issues may concern our relationships, careers, finances, health, and so on. Why do we avoid looking at the memories that remind us of our "open" issues? *Because it is emotionally painful.*

As we discover when we attempt to catch the ox, however, looking is essential. Only when we discover that the pain of being the way we are is greater than the pain of trying to change will we put forth the effort necessary to make significant progress on our inward journey.

In the unconscious, the darkest part of the tunnel, are memories that have been repressed. These memories are deeply buried and may reflect experiences so painful that we were unable to deal with them when they occurred (e.g., sexual abuse or a traumatic accident). In the unconscious we also find thought patterns and belief systems of which we are unaware. These thought patterns may include the tendency to be controlling, manipulative, or antagonistic. Our beliefs may pertain to our individual lives (when, for example, we believe that when we reach our goals we will become perfectly happy, that we have plenty of time before we die, and so on) or to the nature of life itself (when we believe that life is unfair or that there is life after death). We actually never gain direct access to our unconscious. Why is this the case? *Because, by definition, it is unconscious.*

However, there are ways to gain indirect access to our unconscious material. The relationship between our preconscious and our unconscious is like the one between a printer and a computer. A printer's memory can only hold a small amount of information. When a large document is sent from a computer to a printer, the printer holds in memory all that it can, but the balance of the document still resides in the computer's memory. As the document is printed, the printer's memory is able to accept additional information from the computer.

This process continues until the entire document has been transferred.

Our preconscious is like the printer's memory; it can hold only a limited amount of information concerning our issues. As we begin to deal with these issues on the preconscious level, however, we create space for additional information from our unconscious (our "main memory") to arise into consciousness. Many times, the information stored within our preconscious is just the tip of the iceberg. The key to resolving our issues may reside within the unconscious aspect of our minds.

We can use an upward spiral to illustrate the interactive process between the preconscious and unconscious (figure 12).

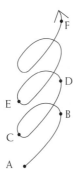

FIGURE 12

At point A we acknowledge the presence of an issue that resides within our preconscious mind. For example, no matter how hard Mary tries, whenever she spends time with John, she inevitably winds up feeling angry. As Mary reflects on her unpleasant encounters with John (i.e., looks at the memories and feelings in her preconscious mind), she realizes that it is John's controlling attitude that makes her upset. This insight is represented by point B.

As a result of this insight, Mary is convinced that she will no longer react with anger the next time she meets with John. When Mary does meet with John, however, anger again arises in her mind. This recurrence of anger is represented by point C.

Mary is not back at point A, although it may feel that way to her. Since she has acknowledged and started to deal with the issue, her preconscious now has more "space" to allow material from the unconscious to arise.

As Mary continues to reflect on the situation, she realizes that the issue with John is really the same issue she has always had with her father, who is also very controlling. (This information came from Mary's unconscious.) She is now at point D in the upward spiral. However, this does not stop Mary from becoming reactive the very next time she sees John (at point E).

As Mary keeps examining her thoughts and feelings related to her situation with John, additional information will be able to move from the unconscious to the preconscious aspect of her mind. This process will continue until Mary gets to the root of the issue and finally spins out of the spiral (at point F).

Sometimes we are so stuck in the drama of our minds that we are unable to work through our issues without outside support. When this occurs it may be helpful to work with a psychotherapist who can help us unravel the psychological tangle in which we are caught. However, the therapist does not have the answers. He or she will rely on the same interactive process between the preconscious and unconscious aspects of our minds to help us discover the underlying cause of our issues.

Our bodies can also act as doorways that open to a greater understanding of what resides within our unconscious. We tend to *somaticize* our psychological issues and therefore experience *psychosomatic* problems. Although these physical symptoms are real and not imagined, they are related to our unconscious thoughts. For example, if we have recurring neck pains, it may be helpful to think about who or what in our lives may be a "pain in the neck." If we always have backaches and there is no physical basis for them, we may want to consider what burden we are carrying around. Stomach aches may point to something we cannot stomach in our lives, and constipation may indicate that we are trying to hold on to something after it is no longer helpful or healthy to do so.

Still another way to uncover unconscious material is through dream interpretation. During sleep, our unconscious mind communicates with us through the use of symbols. However, there are no universal meanings for dream symbols, ones that apply in every case, for every dreamer. A dream needs to be interpreted within the context of the dreamer's life, with the dreamer taking an active part in its interpretation.

Self-understanding, the light which lies on the other side of the tunnel, results from dealing with our issues, maintaining a moment-to-moment awareness of our thought patterns, and replacing our beliefs and assumptions about life with a direct experience of reality. This is, of course, the ultimate goal of the journey.

Our first exercise has four objectives: first, to enable you to catch a glimpse of the material that resides within the preconscious aspect of your mind; second, to reveal the pain that you experience when you look at this material; third, to help you discover how you currently deal with the pain that comes from looking; and finally, to set the stage for a later discussion on effective ways of working through the pain.

EXERCISE: ILLUMINATING SHADOWS

List the five most positive character traits that you possess (e.g., you are generous, patient, loving, truthful, open, flexible, warm, loyal, compassionate, and so forth).

1. _____
2. _____
3. _____
4. _____
5. _____

Now list five character traits directly opposite to the ones you listed (e.g., the opposite of being generous is being selfish, the opposite of patient is impatient, the opposite of loving is hateful or indifferent, the opposite of truthful is dishonest, and so forth).

1. _____
2. _____
3. _____
4. _____
5. _____

The second set of qualities, or character traits, represents your "shadow self." The shadow self resides below the threshold of the conscious mind and possesses qualities directly opposite of the self we present to the world (our persona). It is only when we have moved completely through the tunnel and reach full self-understanding that our shadow side ceases to exist.

It is difficult and painful to recognize or confront our shadow attributes. Because we avoid looking at them, they unconsciously distort our view of the world. We usually wind up projecting our shadow qualities onto others.

When we react to someone emotionally, it may indicate that the other person is displaying a character trait that mirrors one of our own shadow qualities. Because we typically avoid looking at our own shadow traits, it upsets us when we see them in others; it hits too close to home. This is why parents sometimes have a difficult time dealing with children who are just like them!

Acknowledging our shadow is one of the first steps in moving through the tunnel toward self-understanding. The remainder of this exercise will keep you moving in that direction.

EXERCISE: ILLUMINATING SHADOWS (CONTINUED)

Identify and record a specific instance when you recently demonstrated each of the shadow qualities you listed (i.e., the ones opposite to your positive character traits). This may be difficult to do because of the pain that comes from facing them, but work hard at coming up with specifics. For example, if one of your positive qualities is patience, you may remember becoming impatient when you were stuck in traffic, when your child did not complete a homework assignment, and so forth.

1. _____
2. _____
3. _____
4. _____
5. _____

Finally, think about each situation you just recorded. What emotions arise as you remember how you acted in each example you listed (e.g., feelings of guilt, sadness, disappointment, and so on)? Please record each of these emotions.

1. _____
2. _____
3. _____
4. _____
5. _____

These emotional feelings are representative of the pain we experience as we move into our preconscious. Please take some time to consider how you dealt with each of the painful emotions that just arose. Did you tend to hold on to them as a way of punishing yourself for acting "out of character," or did you immediately push them away because of how unpleasant they felt? How we typically respond is important for us to recognize, since it is ultimately not the pain itself, but how we deal with the pain that keeps us from moving through the tunnel to a greater self-understanding.

Most individuals know of only two ways to work with the unpleasant thoughts and feelings that arise when they begin to confront their shadow selves: they either grasp at them or push them away. There are problems with both of these strategies. If we grasp at an experience, it obviously stays with us. If we push the experience away, it still stays with us! The reason is that whatever we resist dealing with persists in the mind. For example, if someone in our family dies and we do not deal with the grief that accompanies the loss, it continues to fester until we finally allow ourselves to complete the grieving process.

An alternative to grasping and pushing is to merely observe what is occurring within our minds with a nonjudgmental or "choiceless" awareness. What we observe in this way arises and passes away without creating a psychological trap for us. The reason that this type of awareness works is that everything is impermanent. If we do not grasp or push away our moment-to-moment experience, it leaves on its own accord. Everything comes to pass, nothing comes to stay. Maintaining a nonjudgmental awareness is the light that guides us through the tunnel to self-understanding.

The capacity to observe nonjudgmentally what is occurring

within the mind can be cultivated through insight meditation. We will complete the instructions for this key process later.

HOW OUR MINDS HAVE BEEN CONDITIONED

Our self-perceptions and overall thinking processes were critically influenced by the communication we received from the significant people in our lives while we were growing up. The process of mental programming during these formative years is conditioned by exposure to repetitive verbal and nonverbal messages.

Several years ago, I went with my family to a wild West theme park in North Carolina. We took a ride on an authentic steam railroad called the Tweetsie. While traveling through the countryside, the train was "attacked" by performers dressed as Native Americans. They were on horseback and they hurled spears and tomahawks at the train in a feigned attempt to stop it or slow it down. Wooden slats had been placed on the windows to protect the passengers from the objects being thrown at the train. However, a tomahawk managed to slip through two slats and hit a child who was sitting across from us. His mother turned to him and, rather than checking to see if he was hurt, said, "Billy, only you! If there were ten thousand kids on this train, you would be the only one hit with a tomahawk!" What kind of self-image do you think that child is forming?

Young children do not always recognize the difference between the truth and a lie and tend to believe what they are consistently told. This is especially true when they hear it from their primary caretakers. When the message negatively focuses on the child's sense of self, the results can be psychologically devastating for years to come. Some common examples of negative self-communication are "you are clumsy," "you are stupid," "you will never amount to anything," "you are just like your no-good father," "you are a disappointment to me."

Comments such as these help create the "tapes" in the child's mind that form the basis of his or her self-image. These tapes continue to play unconsciously throughout the individual's life and are partially responsible for his or her intentions, behaviors, and results.

The unconscious programming of a child's mind is also influenced by indirect communication. For example, if a parent supervises everything a child does, the child gets the message "I am not trustworthy or competent." If the parent exaggerates the child's accomplishments, the child believes that "I must not be good enough as I am." If the parent invalidates the child's feelings or emotions (by saying, for example, "You are not really angry" or "You don't really hate me"), the child believes that his or her feelings are not to be trusted.

The fact that our current self-image is the result of programming is actually good news. This means that it can also be reprogrammed. By consciously using the process of repetitive input, we can reprogram our self-image to reflect what we want to achieve with our lives. The next part of our path explores how this is accomplished.

CONSCIOUSLY REPROGRAMMING THE MIND

In the book *Jonathan Livingston Seagull* by Richard Bach, the seagull Jonathan must learn how to overcome the limitations of his own mental programming in order to discover previously inconceivable dimensions of flight. During the later stages of Jonathan's development, the elder gull Chiang gives him the following advice, "To fly as fast as thought, to anywhere that is, you must begin by knowing that you have already arrived."

Chiang was addressing the issue of self-image. He knew that Jonathan had been programmed to believe in certain limitations. He was advising Jonathan to consciously reprogram his mind by intentionally using the process of repetitive input.

Let's explore the meaning of this advice in terms of how we can consciously reprogram our own minds. As mentioned, consciousness is the moment-to-moment awareness of our sense experiences and cognitive processes. Most people believe that they have one state of consciousness, which maintains a constant awareness of their ever-changing experiences. If we explore our minds deeply, however, we discover discrete acts of consciousness, arising and passing away from moment to moment. Paradoxically, this process occurs so quickly and frequently that it appears not to be happening at all.

To understand this phenomenon, consider a common visual experience. When we go to the movies and watch an interesting film, we get involved in the drama that is taking place on the screen. As the film is being projected, it appears that the actors and actresses are in a constant state of motion. However, if we were to look at the film strip itself, we would discover that there are individual frames, separated by "stop bars." It is due to the speed with which the film is projected on the screen that there appears to be no break in the action. This is analogous to the illusion of a constant state of consciousness.

There is a law in the physical universe that has a counterpart in our psychological world. It states that "two things cannot exist in the same place at the same time." On a psychological level, this means that as each moment of consciousness arises, it can only have one object—one sight, sound, smell, taste, touch, image, or idea—at a time.

Therefore, the way to consciously reprogram our minds, or to change our self-image, is to intentionally hold a thought or image in the mind that reflects how we would like our lives to be, as if we were already living that way. To use Chiang's words, we reach our destination "by knowing that we have already arrived."

When we visualize our self-image in this way, our pro-grammed thoughts and images can no longer remain the objects of our consciousness since we can only have one object of consciousness at a time. Because our actual intentions and behaviors are a reflection of who we think we are and what we believe we are capable of achieving (i.e., our self-image), we start to achieve results that correspond to our new, *intentionally* held, self-image. The positive results, in turn, reinforce our new images until they become habitual and arise spontaneously.

During a previous exercise you listed the goals you have consistently tried to achieve but have been unable to accom-plish. As we discussed, your lack of success could have been due to your self-image being out of alignment with the results you were trying to achieve. The next exercise will help you begin to change your self-image into one that will support the attainment of your goals.

EXERCISE: ATTAINING GOALS

Record the most important goal in each category mentioned in the exercise on page 31–32 (health, finances, career, relationships, and creativity). Write as many details about the goal as you can. For example, if the goal is to buy a house, record the projected cost of the house, the topography of the land where the house will be located, the style of house, the number of rooms, and so forth. It is especially important to project when each goal will be achieved. (Of course, these details can be modified as the goal becomes clearer.)

1. Health:

   a. Most important goal: _____

   b. Details concerning the goal: _____

   _____

   _____

   _____

   _____

2. Finances:

   a. Most important goal: _____

   b. Details concerning the goal: _____

   _____

   _____

   _____

   _____

3. Career:

    a. Most important goal: _____

    b. Details concerning the goal: _____

    _____

    _____

    _____

    _____

4. Relationships:

    a. Most important goal: _____

    b. Details concerning the goal: _____

    _____

    _____

    _____

    _____

5. Creativity:

    a. Most important goal: _____

    b. Details concerning the goal: _____

    _____

    _____

    _____

    _____

Next, take at least sixty seconds to visualize the attainment of each goal. (Make sure you see yourself enjoying each of the goals as part of the picture you create.) *Take time to visualize your goals as often as you can; the results can be extraordinary.*

At this point in the journey it is helpful to begin keeping a journal of the significant thoughts, feelings, or insights that have
arisen in your mind (Journal Entry 1). Keeping such a record
has many benefits:

❖ It provides a forum for releasing some of your
  pent-up feelings or emotions.

❖ You are able to work through (on paper) some of
  the issues residing in your preconscious, which
  creates the space for more repressed material to
  arise to consciousness.

❖ Recording your insights eliminates the need to
  keep replaying them in your mind out of fear of
  forgetting what you have come to understand.

❖ Rereading your earlier entries and noticing how
  much you have grown since recording them gives
  you confidence that you are moving in the right
  direction.

You will be asked to make a journal entry at various times
throughout the rest of your journey. However, you can record
a journal entry any time that it feels appropriate.

Journal Entry 1   *Date:* _____

_____

_____

_____

_____

_____

_____

_____

_____

_____

_____

_____

_____

_____

_____

_____

_____

_____

_____

_____

_____

_____

_____

_____

_____

_____

_____

_____

_____

_____

_____

_____

_____

_____

_____

_____

_____

_____

_____

_____

_____

_____

_____

_____

_____

_____

_____

_____

_____

_____

_____

CHAPTER FOUR

CATCHING THE OX

INSIGHTS: THE UNRESOLVED PAST

The next stage of the journey reaches deeply into the realm of our stored emotions and memories. The insights, obstacles, and practices associated with this phase challenge our ability to find closure with our past and to confront our fears regarding the future.

The first insight we experience at this point is that, to reach the center of our being, we must resolve our open issues. These issues may include residual feelings of anger and resentment, unresolved grief, unsettled conflicts, and fear of losing the people, objects, and circumstances to which we are attached. If we attempt to bypass these issues instead of dealing with them, they will continue to affect every aspect of our lives.

Three individuals once competed to become an apprentice to a wise Sufi master. The Master decided to test each student and to accept as an apprentice the one who demonstrated the greatest wisdom. Each student was given a chicken and asked to take the chicken where no one would see him and kill it. After carrying out this task, they were to return to the teacher and relate what had taken place.

The first student came back in an hour, carrying the dead chicken in his hand. He told the master that he went into the barn, determined that he was alone, and killed the chicken.

The second student, also carrying a dead chicken, returned after two days. He explained that he went to the top of the highest mountain in the region so that he would be sure to have an unobstructed view. After scanning the landscape and seeing no one around, he proceeded to kill the chicken.

The third student returned after one month with the live chicken still in his hand. When the Master asked why he had not killed the chicken as he was instructed to do, the student replied, "Everywhere I went, the chicken saw!"

In a humorous way, this story reminds us that, no matter where we go, we are still under our own watchful gaze, always living in the shadow of those issues in our lives that have never been reconciled. We may succeed in pushing unresolved issues out of our conscious minds, but they will continue to unconsciously distort our perceptions, decisions, and the results that we achieve. The attempt to resolve our issues usually requires that we revisit memories and emotions that are quite painful to experience. It was the unpleasantness of this process that was responsible for our attempt to bypass these issues in the first place. With consistent effort and determination, however, our past will ultimately be put to rest.

The second insight that arises at this stage is how important it is to take a proactive stance toward our fears regarding the future. Our fears are never related to the unknown; we cannot be afraid of something that does not yet exist. We are actually afraid of the loss of the known. By realizing that we can effectively handle any loss that may occur in the future, we paradoxically experience a profound sense of peace in the present. Fear is a wonderful teacher. By learning not to react to it when it arises, we discover an increased ability to live more fully during each moment of our lives.

OBSTACLES: THE TEMPORARY RELIEF OF BYPASSING

Although bypassing our open issues is an ineffective strategy for increasing self-awareness and living a fulfilled life, we may not be able to recognize this since bypassing does offer temporary relief from our psychic pain. We may use drugs, alcohol, or more innocuous activities (such as eating) to alter our moods. Once a mood-altering process is found to be effective, as temporary as its effectiveness may be, it becomes addictive. When the "high" is gone, we focus on getting another fix, sometimes needing to increase the dose to obtain the same results. The momentary release from our pain masks the subtle feeling of despair that always accompanies addiction and is an impediment to realizing the value of directly dealing with our underlying issues.

To break these addictions, we need to clearly understand the actual costs associated with using them as a way to bypass our issues. We have to realize for ourselves that the pain which results from evading our issues inevitably winds up being greater than the pain that comes from actually dealing with them. In other words, we need to experience, firsthand, that bypassing costs too much.

The cost of bypassing will become clearer in the next chapter when we shift our focus from dealing with the content of our minds to learning how our minds operate on a contextual level. The content of our mind is the thoughts, feelings, and images that arise within it from moment to moment. Context, on the other hand, refers to the *process* of thinking, feeling, and imaging that occurs irrespective of the content of those thoughts, feelings, and images. If we attempt to gain some understanding of our mental processes—the contextual level—without first resolving our personal issues, however, our minds will keep getting drawn back to the content level, preventing this more subtle awareness from arising.

This phenomenon is similar to what happens during the sport of bungee jumping. In this activity individuals jump off bridges or other high places with a bungee cord tied to their ankles. As the jumper falls through space, the bungee cord stretches to its fullest extent, then snaps back, taking the individual along with it. Similarly, if we jump into the context level of our minds without having dealt with our content issues, we can only go so far before we are snapped back by the issues to which we are still emotionally tied.

Another cost of bypassing can be seen in the quality of our relationships. Truly meaningful relationships require unconditional acceptance of others as their foundation. As previously discussed, we have a tendency to project our shadow qualities onto the people we meet. Since we do not accept our own shadow qualities, we are certainly not going to accept them when we believe that we see them in others. As we recognize and accept our own shadow qualities, we begin to see people as they really are and find ourselves relating to them in more effective ways.

Once we commit to finding closure with our past, we realize that there are three obstacles that hinder us from doing so. The first obstacle is that we hold on to our anger and resentment. We maintain our anger toward those who have hurt us because we feel justified in doing so. We may feel that forgiveness will be interpreted as condoning abusive behavior, or we may believe that anger gives us power over individuals who have made us feel powerless. Whatever the rationale, clinging to our anger or resentment keeps us emotionally tied to the past.

The second obstacle is that we resist the experience of grief. Life consists of incessant change, and change is always accompanied by loss. We lose our health, youth, loved ones, cherished possessions, jobs, and so forth. We typically resist the grieving process to avoid experiencing the psychic pain that accompanies it. However, we must allow ourselves to grieve if we are to let go of the past and adjust to a life without the people, objects, and circumstances we have lost.

The third obstacle to coming to closure with the past is the existence of unresolved conflicts in our lives. We may avoid dealing with conflict because we are afraid of the consequences. We may believe that conflict is negative and should be avoided at all costs. We may feel that the timing is never quite right. No matter how we justify maintaining our conflicts, however, they still prevent us from moving on with our lives.

Our attachment to certain individuals, objects, or circumstances constitutes the major barrier to mastering our fears regarding the future. As a result of our attachments, we live our lives as if we were walking on thin ice. We psychologically test each decision to see whether it will be safe rather than following our creative impulses or aspirations. The result is a life riddled with fear, lack of self-expression, and unfulfilled dreams. Although it may be a bitter pill to swallow, it is only when we come to realize that we can live a fulfilled life without the individuals, objects, or circumstances to which we are attached that we can truly master our fears regarding the future and reach the fulfillment of our aspirations.

PATH: RESOLVING OUR OPEN ISSUES

We will begin this section of the path with the next set of instructions for insight meditation. As we indicated in our discussion regarding the first set of instructions, it may be helpful to record these directions and play them back during your first few meditation sessions. Leave enough time after each statement so that you can practice what you are being instructed to do. The actual instructions take ten or fifteen minutes, but you can record the sound of a bell at the end of forty-five or sixty minutes to indicate the end of the meditation session. (The original set of instructions is repeated before the addition of new material.)

INSIGHT MEDITATION INSTRUCTIONS

WORKING WITH DISTRACTIONS

❖ Your eyes are closed.

❖ Your mouth is closed and you are breathing
   through your nose.

❖ Feel the touch sensation of your breath as it flows
   in and out of your nostrils at the tip of your nose.
   Some people feel the sensation more strongly
   within the nostrils, while others feel it more on
   the upper lip.

❖ To help you locate where you feel the touch
   sensation of the breath most distinctly, inhale
   deeply and force the air out through your nostrils.
   Wherever you feel the sensation most clearly and
   precisely is the place to keep your attention
   focused for the balance of the meditation period.

❖ Feel the beginning, the middle, and the end of
   every in-breath, and the beginning, the middle,
   and the end of every out-breath.

❖ Sometimes the breath will be short—there is no
   need to make it longer. Sometimes the breath will
   be long—there is no need to make it shorter.
   Sometimes the breath will be erratic—there is no
   need to even it out.

❖ Just become aware of the breath as it goes in and out of the nostrils at the tip of the nose.

❖ Feel the beginning, the middle, and the end of every in-breath, and the beginning, the middle, and the end of every out-breath.

❖ Let the breath breathe itself.

❖ Notice how the quality or experience of every in-breath is different from the quality or experience of every out-breath.

❖ Notice how the quality or experience of every in-breath is different from the quality or experience of every other in-breath, and how the quality or experience of every out-breath is different from the quality or experience of every other out-breath.

❖ Notice the impermanent and changing nature of each breath.

❖ As you focus on the breath, notice that from time to time your attention shifts to other experiences or new objects of awareness. This is not a problem.

❖ Whenever your attention shifts to an object other than the breath, simply become aware of the impermanent and changing nature of that object. Then, gently but firmly, draw your attention back to the touch sensation of the breath.

❖ For example, while you are following the breath you may become aware of a pleasant physical sensation in the body. Becoming aware of that sensation means that you no longer have your attention focused on the breath. Instead of berating yourself for not staying with the breath, merely observe how that sensation also has a beginning, a middle, and an end (i.e., that it is impermanent and constantly changing). Then, gently but firmly, bring your attention back to the breath, your primary object of attention, continuing to watch it rise and fall.

❖ If an unpleasant sensation, such as itching, tightness, or pain arises, and your attention is drawn to that sensation, merely observe its beginning, middle, and end. Then, gently but firmly, draw your attention back to the touch sensation of the breath.

❖ If one of your senses is stimulated and a sense impression such as hearing, smelling, tasting, or touching arises and takes your attention away from the breath, simply observe how that sense experience also has a beginning, a middle, and an end. Then, gently but firmly, return to the breath, watching it rise and fall.

❖ Continue practicing these instructions until the end of the meditation session.

In the original instructions you were told to keep focusing on the breath, no matter what other objects presented themselves to your awareness. This was to enable you to develop the ability to concentrate—a necessary ingredient for the success of this practice. The purpose of this meditation, however, is to gain insight into our moment-to-moment experience. In this second set of instructions, therefore, two additional instructions were added. First, you are told to observe the impermanent and changing nature of each breath. Second, in the event that your attention shifts to a physical sensation (other than the breath) or to a sense experience (other than the sense of sight), you are asked to observe that experience in order to see that it too exhibits the characteristics of impermanence and change.

Please consider the following questions: How did your experience during this meditation session differ from the experiences you had during your prior meditation sessions? Was it easier for you to see the beginning, the middle, or the end phase of each breath? What were the qualitative differences between the in- and out-breaths? What were some of the recurring characteristics of the bodily sensations and sense impressions that you observed?

We will complete the instructions and delve much deeper into the process of insight meditation later in the journey. For now, keep practicing. Try to extend the length of time you sit each day to forty-five or sixty minutes.

To facilitate finding closure with our past, we will engage in three exercises. The first focuses on forgiveness, the second on resolving our grief, and the third on addressing our conflicts.

FORGIVENESS

The antidote to anger and resentment is forgiveness. Most of us find it very difficult to forgive individuals who have hurt us deeply. Why should we forgive them? Although we sometimes make others feel uncomfortable when we express our anger toward them, we are the ones who wind up suffering the most when we do so. Maintaining anger is similar to picking up a red-hot piece of coal to throw at someone—whether we hit our target or not, we are the ones who get burned. Since we cannot give our anger away (nobody really wants it anyway!), the feelings linger and scorch our own minds.

Forgiving does not mean forgetting. When we forgive we still remember the lessons we learned, but without the emotional pain that keeps us anchored to those memories. Forgiving does not indicate that we are condoning an inappropriate or harmful action that someone committed; nor does it mean that we give up our right to justice or to receive better treatment in the future.

You may ask, "Who am I to forgive another person (or myself) for wrongs committed in the past? What gives me that right?" The right to forgive is merely the flip side of the right you have to be angry. One can just as easily ask, "What right do I have to be angry?" It's your choice!

When considering self-forgiveness, there is an important distinction to be made between guilt and regret. Guilt feelings come from repeatedly judging and condemning ourselves after acknowledging the inappropriateness of something we did. As a consequence, we remain angry with ourselves over time. Regret refers to the sorrow we feel when we have committed an unwise action. With regret, we acknowledge our unsuitable behavior, attempt to make amends, and then move on with our lives. Approaching our transgressions with regret is much healthier than living with a sense of guilt and makes it much easier to forgive ourselves.

There is another key point regarding forgiveness. We usually think of people in terms of their bodies, speech, actions, mental processes, or as a combination of these factors. If we look closely, we discover that bodies constantly change, words disappear the moment they are spoken, actions end the instant they are committed, and mental processes incessantly rise and fall away. The people with whom you are angry no longer exist as they were. You are angry only with a memory of how they looked, what they said, what they did, or how they thought. These individuals may still exhibit similar traits, but they are not exactly the same. It is the illusion that nothing has changed that keeps us trapped in the past.

An additional cost of maintaining our anger and resentment can be understood in terms of the quality of love that we are able to express. We can classify love into three categories: sensual, emotional, and unconditional.

Sensual love is the love we have for the objects of our senses. We may "love" flowers, music, or candy. There is, of course, nothing intrinsically wrong with this type of love.

Emotional love is the love we have for another individual. In this kind of love, there is a bonding or deep attachment that takes place between two people. There is nothing intrinsically wrong with this type of love either.

However, both sensual and emotional love are based upon the pleasant feelings we experience when we are in the presence of certain individuals or sense objects. Consequently, we no longer love those individuals or objects the moment we stop experiencing these pleasant feelings. We may not hate the individuals or objects (unless the feelings we begin to experience are distinctly unpleasant), but we will no longer feel drawn to them.

Unconditional love, on the other hand, is an expression of love that is not based upon pleasant feelings. It is instead unlimited. Anyone who meets an individual with unconditional love can experience its presence, and the one who expresses it becomes a loving person. It is similar to a flower that emits its fragrance without regard to the "worth" of those who smell it.

The ultimate cost of maintaining anger and hatred is our inability to become truly loving individuals (although many of us may believe that we already are). Holding on to conditions in our mind for when we can let go of anger and forgive others naturally precludes our expression of love from becoming unconditional. The cost of maintaining anger and hatred is too high for anyone.

You are now going to take a "guided imagery forgiveness tour." The stops along the way will be the places where forgiveness may not as yet have entered your heart. Be careful not to judge yourself for what you may be unable to do at this time—that only compounds the very issues you are trying to resolve. The more layered your anger, or the deeper your hurt, the more extensive your work will need to be.

Some catharsis or emotional release is both helpful and inevitable. If you find yourself being carried away by your emotions during any phase of this (or any other) exercise, use your breath as a centering device, as you did while practicing insight meditation.

As with the instructions for insight meditation, it might be helpful to record these directions. Leave enough time in between each statement to comfortably move through the process. As an alternative, you and a friend can take turns reading the instructions aloud and completing the forgiveness exercise.

EXERCISE: EXPRESSING FORGIVENESS

FORGIVING SOMEONE YOU ARE ANGRY WITH

❖ Imagine a room where the only furnishings are two chairs facing each other. You are sitting in one chair and the chair opposite you is empty. Behind the empty chair is a door.

❖ Suddenly, there is a knock at the door, and you ask the person to come in. Into the room enters someone you have been angry with for a long time. It may be a person who is currently in your life, someone from your past, or even an individual who is no longer alive.

❖ Do not choose yourself as this person for this first part of the exercise.

❖ If several people come to mind and try to enter the room, allow in only the person for whom you have the greatest feeling of anger.

❖ Tell the others that they will have another opportunity to meet with you in the future.

❖ Ask the person to sit in the chair facing you.

❖ Carefully look at that individual. Notice what he or she is wearing. Look at his or her facial characteristics and the way his or her hair is styled.

❖ Now look directly into that person's eyes. Imagine that he or she really desires your forgiveness.

❖ You are not condoning or approving the individual's behavior—you are just trying to let go of the anger, resentment, and hatred in your own heart.

❖ Now say to that person, "I forgive you. I forgive you for the hurtful things you said to me." (Remember the hurtful things that were said and forgive that person for having said them.)

❖ "I forgive you for the lies you told me and for those you told to other people about me." (Remember the lies that person told and forgive him or her for having told those lies.)

❖ If you get carried away emotionally, remember to come back to your breath.

❖ "I forgive you for all that you have done to hurt me." (Remember any physical and/or emotional abuse and forgive that person for having acted in those ways.)

❖ If you feel physical or emotional pain as you remember, allow yourself to experience the pain without resisting it. If you get carried away by your emotions, refocus on your breath.

❖ "I forgive you for betraying me."

❖ "I forgive you for all the threats you made in an attempt to intimidate me."

❖ "I forgive you for not forgiving me."

❖ "I forgive you for not treating me in the same way as you treated others."

❖ "I forgive you for judging me so harshly and thinking so badly of me."

❖ It is difficult to forgive when you feel that someone has hurt you without cause. Keep remembering that this process is for you to finally be free of the emotions and memories that bind you to the past and prevent you from completing your journey. Just move at your own pace without judging yourself for any difficulty you may have completing this process.

❖ The person sitting opposite you is not the same person who treated you so harshly. Who the person was then is not who the person is now. So much has changed for both you and that individual—even if it was yesterday that he or she hurt you. By perpetuating your anger, you only punish yourself!

❖ Look the person in the eyes and say, "I forgive you." Let your heart open to the person just a bit more and offer this one final thought of forgiveness.

❖ Allow any feelings of emotional freedom that may have come from this process of forgiveness to arise.

❖ As the person stands up to leave, if it is comfortable for you to do so, hug the person before he or she departs.

❖ The person now walks toward the door, opens it, and leaves.

❖ Take a deep, cleansing breath—someone else is waiting.

FORGIVING YOURSELF

❖ Again you hear a knock at the door and respond by inviting the person to come in. As the person enters the room, you realize that it is yourself who has entered. Ask yourself to sit in the chair which faces you.

❖ Carefully look at yourself. Notice what you are wearing. Study the shape of your body. Look at your hair. Closely observe your facial character-istics. Now look directly into your own eyes. Acknowledge how much you want to be able to forgive yourself for all your past misdeeds, so that you can finally move on with your life.

❖ Now, calling yourself by name, say "_____, I forgive you."

❖ Now say to yourself, "I forgive you for the hurtful things you have said to others." (Recall the hurtful things you have said to others over the years and forgive yourself.)

❖ "I forgive you for the hurtful things you have said to yourself." (Remember the hurtful things you have said to yourself over the years and forgive yourself.)

❖ "I forgive you for all the lies you have told." (Think about the lies you have told over the years and forgive yourself for having told them.)

❖ "I forgive you for all that you have done to hurt other people throughout your life, no matter how terrible those things may have been." (Recall the hurtful things you have done throughout your life and forgive yourself for having done them. There is no longer any need to carry around feelings of guilt.)

❖ If you feel physical or emotional pain as you remember, allow yourself to experience the pain without resisting it. If you get carried away by your emotions, refocus on your breath.

❖ Forgive yourself for not taking a stand and letting others mistreat you.

❖ Forgive yourself for being human and having imperfections.

❖ It is difficult to forgive ourselves when we have been carrying around our anger and self-hatred for so long. Move at your own pace without judging yourself for how hard it is for you to complete this process.

❖ Remember that this process is a gift to yourself so that you can finally be free of the emotions and memories that bind you to the past and prevent you from completing your journey.

❖ The person sitting opposite you is not the same person who said or did all those things in the past. Who you were then is not who you are now. So much has changed for you since that time—even if it was this morning that you were hurtful to someone.

❖ If you still possess the same negative characteristics, you need to work on changing them. By perpetuating your anger or self-hatred, however, you punish yourself for things you have not yet done.

❖ Calling yourself by name, say "_____, I forgive you."

❖ You are not condoning or approving of what you have done in the past. You are just trying to let go of the anger, resentment, and self-hatred in your heart.

❖ Let your heart open to yourself just a bit more and offer yourself one final thought of forgiveness.

❖ Allow any feelings of emotional freedom that may have come from the process of self-forgiveness to arise.

❖ See yourself standing up. If you are comfortable with doing so, give yourself a hug. Now open the door and see yourself leaving the room.

❖ Take a deep, cleansing breath and open your eyes.

Please open your journal (Journal Entry 2) and record the thoughts, feelings, images, and insights that arose during the forgiveness exercise. You can use the following questions as a way to explore your experience.

❖ When you thought about someone you were angry with and needed to forgive, did more than one person come to mind? What does that say to you?

❖ Were you surprised by any of the individuals who came to mind? Did you think that you had already forgiven some of those people? What does that suggest to you?

❖ What thoughts and feelings did you experience as you attempted to forgive the person who came into the room?

❖ Were you able to forgive that person? If not, what were the barriers that prevented you from being able to do so? (These barriers must be recognized to move beyond them.)

❖ What thoughts and feelings did you experience as you attempted to forgive yourself?

❖ Were you able to forgive yourself? If not, what were the barriers to being able to do so? (These barriers must be recognized in order to move beyond them.)

Journal Entry 2   *Date:* _____

RESOLVING GRIEF

Grief is the normal psychological response to the experience of loss. It arises after a loss occurs or when we anticipate a loss ("anticipatory" grief). Our losses can be obvious (e.g., the death of a loved one, getting fired from a job, the breakup of a marriage) or more subtle (e.g., loss of independence when we become caretakers to elderly parents, loss of youth, or loss of the opportunity to fulfill a dream).

The grieving process enables us to release our attachments to the people, objects, or circumstances that were lost. We may resist grieving for many reasons: not wanting to face the painful feelings associated with grief, not wanting to face the reality of the loss, or not wanting to reawaken the memory of a prior loss, among others. However, short-circuiting the grieving process leaves us with unresolved grief. As a result, we remain emotionally bound to our losses.

The way we grieve is an individual matter. It depends primarily upon our personal history and what our losses represent to us. For example, losing a spouse may also represent the loss of a friend, a lover, and a sense of security. The loss of a breast due to cancer may also represent the cutting off of one's femininity, beauty, and youth. In spite of the individual differences, for most people the grieving process is divided into three stages: shock, recognition, and recovery.

While in *shock*, the individual is unable to come to terms with the reality and potential consequences of his or her loss. Although the person understands intellectually what has occurred, an unconscious denial takes place. Typical remarks made by individuals going through this stage include "I don't believe that this is really happening," "It can't be true," and "It seems like a dream." As a result of this denial, one may "forget" the loss and attempt to speak to someone who died as if he or she were in the next room or expect the person to come home at the usual time. Emotional blunting or the feeling of numbness is typical at this point.

During *recognition* the physical reality of the loss is finally acknowledged. In an unconscious attempt to maintain some link with the person, object, or circumstance, one may become preoccupied with thoughts of the past and keep relating stories of what it was like before the loss occurred.

During this stage the person is in emotional turmoil and experiences a great deal of pain. The grieving individual may also feel guilt, anger, depression, and a deep sense of longing or despair. Physical symptoms include headaches, nausea, tightness in the throat, heaviness in the chest, and an empty feeling in the pit of the stomach.

In *recovery* the oppressive pain begins to subside. The loss is now accepted as part of the person's life. The physical sensations of heaviness begin to lift and one's energy starts to return. The individual is now able to emotionally reinvest himself or herself in new relationships and activities.

Denial, recognition, and recovery are natural stages of grieving. There is no right length of time in which to move through each stage. If we resist grieving, however, we continue to remain emotionally tied to the past. The following exercise is designed to enable you to find closure with your unresolved grief.

EXERCISE: RESOLVING GRIEF

This exercise may call forth painful memories. Try to soften into the pain without resistance. If you get emotionally carried away, come back to your breath.

If any part of this experience becomes overwhelming and you have to stop, please do not judge yourself for having to do so. You can always return to the exercise at another time.

Although this exercise is oriented toward the loss of individuals in your life, it can also be used to deal with the loss of cherished objects or circumstances.

Record your most significant losses under the following two categories:

1. Individuals who have died:

_____

_____

_____

_____

_____

2. Individuals who have left you (e.g., a parent who abandoned your family, a child who moved out, or a spouse who wanted a divorce):

_____

_____

_____

_____

Choose the one loss from these lists with which you have had the greatest difficulty in dealing. (At a later date, you can

complete this process for each of your unresolved losses.)
Answer the following questions regarding that loss:

❖ How did you find out that the loss occurred?

_____

_____

_____

❖ Did you know that the loss was about to occur?

_____

❖ Do you feel partially responsible for the loss occurring?

_____

❖ (If yes to previous question) In what ways do you feel
responsible?

_____

_____

_____

_____

_____

❖ In what ways has your life been affected by the loss?

_____

_____

_____

_____

_____

❖ What has been the most painful part of the loss (e.g., the deathbed experience, the suddenness of the loss, your feeling of being partially responsible for the loss, the recognition that your life will never be the same, your never having told the person how much you loved him or her, your never having apologized for something you did or said, or some other unresolved issue with the person)?

_____

_____

_____

_____

_____

_____

_____

_____

_____

_____

_____

❖ What does the loss represent to you (the loss of acceptance, the loss of love, the loss of self-respect, the loss of a dream, and so forth)?

_____

_____

_____

_____

_____

_____

_____

❖ What unfinished business do you have with the person you lost (e.g., not having told the person how much you loved him or her, the need to apologize, that you never said goodbye, or that you never resolved an abuse issue)?

_____

_____

_____

_____

_____

_____

_____

_____

_____

_____

❖ Describe in detail the physical, emotional, and psychological pain you have experienced due to this loss.

_____

_____

_____

_____

_____

_____

_____

_____

_____

_____

_____

_____

The final part of this exercise will be another guided imagery process. As before, you may want to tape the directions and play them back, giving yourself enough time to complete each phase of the process.

❖ Bring the memory of the person you have been writing about into your mind.

❖ As you engage in the following dialogue, imagine the person responding to you in the ways you prefer.

❖ Tell the person how your life has been affected by the loss.

❖ Explain to the person what the most painful part of the loss experience has been for you.

❖ Describe what this loss represented to you.

❖ Express the emotions with which you have been dealing.

❖ Complete your unfinished business with this person (e.g., apologize for something you did, express how much you really loved him or her, say goodbye).

❖ If you feel the need, ask for and receive forgiveness.

❖ Finally, ask for and receive permission to move on with your life.

❖ Allow any feelings of emotional freedom that may have come from moving through the grieving process to arise.

❖ Say goodbye, take a deep cleansing breath, and open your eyes.

Please open your journal (Journal Entry 3), and record the thoughts, feelings, images, and insights that arose during this exercise. You can use the following questions as a way of exploring your experience. There are no right or wrong answers.

❖ Were you surprised by the loss with which you chose to work?

❖ (If yes) Why were you surprised by that choice?

❖ Which memory regarding this loss was the most difficult or painful for you to face?

❖ What does that painful memory represent or symbolize to you?

❖ With which emotions were you dealing?

❖ Did any of your unfinished business surprise you?

❖ (If yes) Why were you surprised?

❖ Were you able to complete your unfinished business?

❖ (If not) Aside from this being an exercise that took place only in your mind, what were the impediments to completing your unfinished business?

❖ Did you get permission to move on with your life?

❖ (If not) What were the barriers to doing so? (It is important that these barriers are recognized and worked through.)

❖ Which other losses are you committed to working through?

❖ What are you feeling right now?

Journal Entry 3   *Date:* _____

_____

_____

_____

_____

_____

_____

_____

_____

_____

_____

_____

_____

_____

_____

_____

_____

_____

_____

_____

_____

_____

_____

_____

_____

_____

_____

_____

ADDRESSING CONFLICTS

The final exercise concerned with gaining closure with our past addresses the conflicts we have with the significant people in our lives. Conflict refers to the mental struggles that result from apparently incompatible or opposing needs. Interpersonal conflict can arise over any topic or circumstance: relationships, parenting, finances, sexuality, religion, and so forth.

We may delay dealing with our conflicts by telling ourselves that we have plenty of time to resolve them. But life is quite uncertain, and our circumstances may change so suddenly and dramatically that we lose the opportunity to gain closure on these issues. This leaves us with the thought "if only…," which can plague us for the rest of our lives. As with anger and grief, unresolved conflicts keep us emotionally bound to the past.

To assist you in recognizing your conflicts and in making specific commitments to resolve them, we will engage in another exercise. Since part of this exercise involves guided imagery, you may want to tape the directions and play them back, giving yourself enough time to complete each phase of the process.

EXERCISE: SETTLING CONFLICTS

❖ Close your eyes.

❖ Imagine that you are driving your car.

❖ Without warning, an automobile swerves into your lane and crashes head-on into yours.

❖ You are thrown from your car and find yourself on the ground, unable to move or speak.

❖ You are bleeding and are in excruciating pain, but you cannot call out.

❖ You are in a silent panic as you realize that you may die or be paralyzed for the rest of your life.

❖ You are brought to the shock trauma unit of a hospital, where the doctors ask questions to which you are unable to respond.

❖ The doctors finally recognize the pain that you are in and give you a shot of morphine.

❖ As the pain subsides and you begin to feel groggy, you look up and see all the significant people in your life looking down at you, with love, sorrow, and despair in their eyes.

❖ Look at each of their faces.

❖ Determine exactly who is there.

❖ Open your eyes and create a list of everyone who was at your bedside.

_____

_____

_____

_____

❖ Close your eyes once more.

❖ Picture the first person you placed on your list.

❖ You may never again have the opportunity to communicate with this individual.

❖ What conflicts do you have with this person that you wish you would have resolved before this moment?

❖ Please open your eyes.

❖ In the lines provided below, record that person's name, the conflicts you have with that person, and a date by which you are committed to resolving these conflicts. (Although we want to resolve these conflicts as quickly as possible, we need to make sure the timing of our communication is appropriate.)

Name	Conflicts	Date
——	————————	——
——	————————	——
——	————————	——
——	————————	——
——	————————	——
——	————————	——
——	————————	——
——	————————	——
——	————————	——
——	————————	——
——	————————	——

❖ Continue this process of calling each person to mind, reviewing the conflicts you have with him or her, recording these conflicts, and committing to a date by which they will be resolved.

❖ For the people you are unable to contact (individuals who have died, moved away, and so on) or prefer not to contact (e.g., a former spouse or a person from your past who was abusive), you can work through the conflicts mentally. Pretend that you are engaging in a dialogue with each of these people and visualize a successful resolution to each conflict.

❖ Finally, transfer your commitments to your regular "to do" list or calendar, so they will stay at the forefront of your mind until they are fulfilled.

Please open your journal (Journal Entry 4) and record the thoughts, feelings, images, and insights that arose during this exercise. You can use the following questions as a way of exploring your experience. There are no right or wrong answers.

❖ Were you surprised by the individuals who appeared at your bedside?

❖ (If yes) Why did their appearance surprise you?

❖ Did any conflicts arise in your mind that you thought were already resolved?

❖ (If yes) Why do you think they arose again?

❖ Were there any commitments to resolving your conflicts that you were unable to make?

❖ (If yes) Why do you believe you were unable to make those commitments? (This is important to understand so that the barriers can be worked through.)

❖ What concerns do you have about what will happen when you attempt to gain closure with some or all of the people on your list?

❖ How will you deal with those concerns?

Journal Entry 4   *Date:* _____

CONFRONTING FEAR

The last trap we have to set to catch the ox is to confront the very fears that we have tended to avoid. As we discussed, we need to deal with our fears regarding the future proactively, rather than reacting to them whenever they enter our minds.

Our fears are never related to the unknown. We cannot be afraid of something that we know nothing about. We are afraid of the loss of the known (our relationships, possessions, money, acceptance from others, self-respect, confidence, and security). The basis of our fears is the belief that if we lose the things we are attached to, we will not be able to handle those losses. In other words, we fear that we will never get through our pain or that our lives will never feel complete or fulfilling. The following exercise will enable you to realize that, no matter what losses you may encounter, you *can* get through the pain, and your life *can* feel complete and fulfilling.

This is one of the most emotionally painful and powerful exercises within this book. Please do not skip it; its value cannot be overstated. If you successfully complete the exercise, your future decisions will be based upon your deepest visions rather than your greatest fears.

EXERCISE: CONFRONTING FEARS

❖ Obtain ten index cards.

❖ On each card, write the name of one individual,
   object, or circumstance that you love or highly
   value. Individuals may include parents, children,
   significant others, relatives, friends, or pets.
   Objects may include jewelry, paintings, articles of
   clothing, and so forth. Circumstances may include
   good health, success, or life itself.

❖ Record only one entry per card.

❖ Stack the cards in order of importance, placing
   the least important on the top and the most
   important on the bottom.

❖ Take the top card (the one containing what is of
   least value to you) in your hand and imagine
   permanently losing that person, object, or
   circumstance. Imagine a scenario that would force
   you to face never being able to experience that
   person, object, or circumstance again (e.g.,
   imagine that your child is dying, that something
   which cannot be replaced is stolen, or that you
   permanently lose your health).

❖ Spend some time saying goodbye to the person,
   object, or circumstance that you are in the process
   of losing.

❖ After you have visualized with clarity and certainty that you will never again be able to experience the person, object, or circumstance that you indicated on the first card, rip the card up and put it aside.

❖ Close your eyes and see yourself grieving for that loss.

❖ Finally, visualize your life being as being fulfilled, happy, and complete without that person, object, or circumstance. You can imagine any scenario you like (starting another significant relationship, spending more time in creative self-expression, buying a new house, and so forth).

Of course some losses, such as the loss of a parent or a child, will be more difficult to work through. However, it can be done. There are people who have experienced these kinds of losses and continued living fulfilled lives blessed with peace and joy. Remember, if you can imagine yourself achieving the results, it will be possible for you to manifest the behaviors necessary to realize those results.

❖ Now complete the same process for each of the cards.

❖ If strong emotional feelings arise, use your breath as your centering device.

❖ Be careful not to judge yourself if you find your-self unable to complete this process due to intense emotional reactions. You can always come back to this process at a later point.

Please open your journal (Journal Entry 5) and record the thoughts, feelings, images, and insights that arose during this exercise. You can use the following questions as a way of exploring your experience. There are no right or wrong answers.

❖ If you were to do this again, would you reorder the cards or change their contents?

❖ (If yes) Why would you make those changes?

❖ Although the reason may seem obvious, why do you think it was more difficult to deal with the people, objects, or circumstances at the bottom of your pile of cards?

❖ Were you able to see yourself in a situation where you "lost" the person, object, or circumstance you placed on each of your cards?

❖ (If not) Why do you think you were unable to do so?

❖ Were you able to complete the grieving process?

❖ (If not) Why do you think that this was the case?

❖ Were you able to visualize a happy, fulfilled, and complete life without the people, objects, or circumstances that you placed on your cards?

❖ (If not) What were the barriers?

❖ If you were unable to complete the exercise due to your resistance or emotional responses, when are you committed to doing so?

❖ If you are unwilling to make such a commitment, why do you think that this is the case?

Journal Entry 5   *Date:* _____

_____

_____

_____

_____

_____

_____

_____

_____

_____

_____

_____

_____

_____

_____

_____

_____

_____

_____

_____

_____

_____

_____

_____

_____

_____

_____

_____

CHAPTER FIVE

TAMING THE OX

INSIGHTS: BECOMING AWARE

In an earlier discussion, we introduced the concept that we are controlled only by those patterns of thinking, imaging, and feeling of which we are unaware. When these unconscious patterns emerge we react according to our prior conditioning or programming. Even positive thinking will not help us gain control of these patterns. Although positive thoughts produce positive results, they are not better than negative thoughts when it comes to taming our minds. Although we may be reacting in more effective ways, if we are unaware that these unconscious patterns have arisen, we are still being controlled by them.

One insight that arises at this stage of our journey is that in order to tame the ox we need to stop identifying with our individual thoughts, images, and feelings and instead begin observing the process of thinking, imaging, and feeling. In other words, we need to shift from grasping at the contents of our minds to learning how our minds operate on a contextual level.

A second insight is that, in order to be successful, we must dedicate every aspect of our lives to reaching this goal. A tightrope walker must pay close attention to his or her every step or risk a fall. In the same way, if we become distracted by goals that are at cross purposes to our present journey, we will lose our balance and fail to achieve the inner peace and enlightenment we seek.

OBSTACLES: PERCEPTUAL DISTORTIONS

The first obstacle to taming the ox is the presence of perceptual distortions deeply embedded within our minds. Perceptual distortions are erroneous ideas or beliefs about the true nature of our experience. These distortions keep us identified with the contents of our minds and make it difficult for us to experience our psychological processes on a contextual level. There are three primary perceptual distortions:

1. The belief that what we experience is permanent.

2. The belief that our experiences can provide us with a lasting sense of satisfaction.

3. The belief that there is an unchanging *self* which is part of, in control of, or aware of our moment-to-moment experiences.

Another obstacle to taming the ox is the multiplicity of goals and intentions that dominate our minds and diffuse our efforts to achieve self-mastery. We typically divide our lives (and our minds) into neat compartments. Certain times of the day are devoted to specific activities, such as working, eating, or engaging in recreational activities. These discrete times usually have separate and distinct goals associated with them. We work to earn money or to express ourselves, we eat to enjoy the taste of food or to sustain our bodies, and we engage in recreational activities to relax, have fun, or to keep in shape.

If we examine our experience throughout the day, we may discover that our compartments are not airtight and that many of these discrete times are actually in competition with one another. For example, you may be spending time with your family but find yourself thinking about work. This type of compartmentalizing diffuses our energy and makes it difficult for us to achieve our mundane goals, let alone self-mastery.

The key to generating enough energy and momentum to successfully reach the center of being is to unify all the diverse aspects of our lives. By orienting them all toward the goal of achieving self-mastery, we transform each moment of life into an opportunity to further our inward journey. This is accomplished by cultivating *clear comprehension*, which we will address later in this chapter.

PATH: GAINING PERSPECTIVE

This phase of our journey begins with a series of exercises designed to give you a direct experience of how you are controlled by the mental constructs you identify with and how essential it is, therefore, for you to gain a "contextual" perspective on your mind. These exercises will also illustrate how this lack of perspective is actually responsible for creating the stress that you experience.

We will be using the words *circumstance* and *perception* throughout these exercises. A circumstance is the actual state of affairs, regardless of our interpretations about what is occurring. A perception, on the other hand, is our point of view concerning an experience and does not necessarily reflect the reality of what is taking place. To illustrate this distinction, we can use the example of a painting hanging on a wall. By describing the painting as either beautiful or unattractive, we are communicating our perceptions. The actual circumstance is simply that there is a painting hanging on a wall.

EXERCISE: DISCOVERING THE SOURCE OF ALL STRESS

Under each of the following categories, please list circumstances that you believe create stress for you. List as many as
you can. Be as specific as possible in identifying the exact cause
of the stress in each situation. The following are examples of
what others have recorded under each category:

Home

1. "The clutter my husband leaves around the house"

2. "Having to mow the lawn on weekends"

Work

1. "Telephone calls when working on an important project"

2. "Being on-call and never knowing when I'll be paged"

Finances

1. "The amount of money it takes to pay for my daughter's
   college"

2. "The amount of taxes taken from my paycheck"

Relationships

1. "My wife's jealousy"

2. "My mother still trying to control my life"

1. Home

_____
_____
_____
_____
_____

2. Work

_____
_____
_____
_____
_____

3. Finances

_____
_____
_____
_____
_____

4. Relationships

_____
_____
_____
_____
_____

To complete this first exercise you must analyze your statements and determine whether or not those circumstances *truly* create stress for you. To conduct an effective analysis, you will need the groundwork provided by the exercises and discussions that follow. We will return to this first exercise shortly.

Please begin the next exercise by reading the following story:

A married couple live in a house they adore. They love the size of the house, the shape of the rooms, the amount of closet space, and even the view from their windows. One day the husband is offered a promotion which, if accepted, would require moving out of state. The decision is made to accept the promotion, and the couple sells their house. The couple who purchase the house become dissatisfied with it shortly after moving in. They hate the size of the house, the shape of the rooms, the amount of closet space, and even the view from their windows; yet, everything is exactly the same as it had been for the previous owners. The longer the new owners live in the house, the more stress they experience.

What do you believe was the actual source of stress for the second couple?

To answer this question we need to discuss the concept of intrinsic properties. "Intrinsic" means that a specific characteristic or property belongs to some person, place, or thing, that it is an essential part of its makeup. If that characteristic or property did not exist, therefore, neither would the person, place, or thing. For example, intrinsic to a rock is the property of hardness. You may have the elements that comprise a rock, but if you do not have hardness, you do not have a rock.

In terms of our exercise, is a house ever intrinsically large or small? Are the shapes of rooms ever intrinsically perfect? Is the amount of closet space ever intrinsically adequate? Is a view ever intrinsically beautiful? The answer to all these questions is, of course, no. Large, small, adequate, inadequate, beautiful, and unattractive are all relative concepts and are based upon our own perceptions. In fact, the only true statement you can ever make about a house is that it is a house! Any other statement would be a reflection of our own point of view.

Returning to our story, if you ask the second couple what created their stress, they would most likely answer that it was the house (i.e., the circumstance). However, this answer would not be accurate. The actual source of their stress was believing that their perceptions regarding the size of the house, the shape of the rooms, the amount of closet space, and the view from their windows were intrinsic to the house itself.

A circumstance, such as a house, is always neutral and incapable of creating stress. Stress comes from identifying with our perceptions and therefore believing them to be an intrinsic part of our circumstances.

The next exercise further clarifies how our unconscious patterns control us, and how our lack of perspective creates the stress that we experience. Please pay careful attention to all the details so that you can answer a series of questions at the end of the story.

John and Mary have been married for over twenty years. They have three teenage children—two daughters and a son. John has been working for the same company for ten years; Mary is not employed. They live in a house which they believe is too small for their needs, since it only has two bedrooms. John and Mary sleep in one bedroom, their daughters share the second bedroom, and their son sleeps on the couch in the living room.

To buy a larger home they would have to do two things. First, they would have to take every penny from the sale of their current home and use the money for a down payment on their new home. Second, they would have to use all of their savings to pay for closing costs. This would potentially leave them without any money for a rainy day, so they remain where they are.

One day John goes into work and his manager asks him to come into his office. He tells John that he has been doing a great job and that in three weeks he will be given a promotion and a substantial raise. When John goes home, he tells Mary the good news. They talk it over and decide to buy a new home as quickly as possible.

That weekend, they find their "dream house." They make an offer to the owners, which is immediately accepted. The following weekend John and Mary hold an "open house." A couple makes an offer on their house, which John and Mary gladly accept. During the third weekend, they close the sale and purchase the new house. As they already knew, John and Mary have to use all the money from the sale of their house for the down payment on the new home and all of their savings for closing costs.

John goes into work on Monday morning looking forward to meeting with his manager and finding out exactly how large a raise he will be receiving. When his manager sees John, he immediately asks him to come into his office. Before John can utter a word, his manager says, "John, let me come right to the point. I have to make some changes. I'm sorry, but you're fired!"

EXERCISE: ENCOUNTERING PERCEPTIONS

Next to each of the following statements, write a C if you believe that the statement reflects a circumstance, or a P if it reflects a perception.

1. John was fired from his job. _____

2. John will not be able to afford the payments on his new home. _____

3. John will have no money until he gets a new job. _____

4. Mary will be upset when she hears the news. _____

The answer to the first question is C (i.e. circumstance), since being fired is the actual state of affairs, regardless of how John may choose to interpret what has occurred. The answers to questions two, three, and four are all P (i.e., perception), since these statements reflect John's point of view concerning his present situation—not necessarily the reality of what is taking place.

How can that be? The story indicated that John spent all the money from the sale of his home on the down payment for the new house, and that he spent every penny from his savings for closing costs. What spouse would not be upset when he or she heard that kind of news?

All this may be true, but the statements are still perceptions. What is the one word in each statement that turns that statement into a perception rather than a circumstance?

It is the word "will"!

Why does "will" turn the statements into perceptions? "Will" refers to the future. Although an outcome may "probably," "almost certainly," and "most likely" be true, it does not mean that it *will* be true!

It is possible for John to get a better job than he had before, for Mary to get a job, for John to get severance pay, or even for John and Mary to inherit money. It is also possible that Mary never liked John's job and secretly felt that he could do better. It is not a question of how "probable" these possibilities are. The point is that these possibilities, along with other scenarios that we have not even mentioned, can indeed take place. *We do not know what will happen in the future, no matter how likely a particular outcome may be.*

If either John or Mary experienced any stress after John was fired, it would not come from John being fired (i.e., the circumstance). It would stem from the belief that their negative perceptions regarding the consequences of being fired were intrinsic to the act of being fired. They would be identifying with, and therefore reacting to, the content of their thoughts.

You may know of individuals who were happy about being fired because they were able to collect unemployment insurance or because it created the impetus for them to go into their own business. I am not suggesting that being fired should be perceived as good or as an opportunity. I am also not stating that John and Mary will have no stress. All I am saying is that being fired is a neutral experience and is not capable of creating stress in and of itself.

At this point we are ready to complete the first exercise. You were asked to list the circumstances that you believe create stress for you. Please turn to the list you generated and look at each item. Do you still believe that the circumstances you described "in and of themselves" create stress for you?

If you do, ask yourself the question, "If I thought that any or all of those circumstances were positive and I looked forward to experiencing them, would they still create stress for me?"

Remember that we are not asking you to change your perceptions. We are only questioning whether a change in your perception alters the capacity of circumstances to create stress for you.

This is not an easy concept to grasp. We have believed in the intrinsic negativity of certain circumstances for so long that it is difficult for the mind to move from content to context—from habitually identifying with our thoughts and feelings to objectively observing our own beliefs.

As we have stated, no circumstance is intrinsically positive or negative; the circumstance is just the state of affairs that exists at the moment. If you carefully reflect on each of the circumstances you recorded, you would probably be able to think of a situation where someone could have a positive perception of that same circumstance. For example, in considering some of our earlier illustrations:

❖ Some people enjoy mowing their lawn.

❖ A person does not feel disturbed by telephone calls if he or she is looking forward to receiving them.

❖ There is an organization in this country comprised of individuals who would like to see taxes raised.

❖ For some, jealousy is a sign that the other person still cares.

By changing our negative perceptions into positive ones, our stress disappears. The conclusion, however, is not necessarily that we should change our perceptions. It is simply that circumstances, in and of themselves, do not create the stress that we experience. It is difficult to acknowledge the truth of this conclusion because it requires that we stop playing the victim, and begin taking responsibility for the quality of our lives. Once we concede that it is our own perceptions that create our stress, we can no longer point our finger at anyone or anything outside of our own minds as being the source of the stress that we experience. Not many individuals are willing or able to accept that level of responsibility for their lives.

Once we are aware of what our perceptions are, we can consciously respond, rather than unconsciously react to them. There are three possible ways of responding:

Change our perceptions. We would choose this alternative if our perceptions were unrealistic or self-limiting. For example, the beliefs that we must be loved and respected by everyone and that we must be perfectly competent in everything we do cannot be achieved. Therefore, holding to these perceptions only brings feelings of inadequacy and frustration.

Keeping our perceptions and changing the circumstance. We would pick this alternative if our perceptions were realistic. For example, if one was in an abusive relationship and had a perception that the relationship should be ended, or that counseling of some sort was needed, this perception would be reasonable. By changing the circumstance (i.e., ending the relationship or going for counseling), the individual would most likely feel safer and experience greater self-esteem.

Recognizing our perceptions and letting them pass without changing them or attempting to alter our circumstances. This alternative would be chosen if our perceptions were based upon emotional reactions to a circumstance which had just occurred. For example, if someone said something offensive, and you wanted to say something hurtful in return because you had a perception that you were justified in doing so, you would merely recognize your perception and allow it to pass.

Of course, to "respond" in any of these three ways, we have to first become aware of what our perceptions are. This type of awareness is cultivated through the practice of insight meditation. To derive the optimum benefits from this form of meditation, we need to understand and cooperate with the principles that make the process so effective. These principles are referred to as paying *bare attention,* cultivating *momentary concentration,* and observing *the true characteristics of our experience.*

BARE ATTENTION

Paying bare attention is examining our experiences during meditation with an attention which is bare of judgment, bare of decision, and bare of commentary. It is the direct observation of our minds and bodies without any interference from our cognitive processes.

Bare of judgment means not making a determination as to whether the experiences we have during meditation are right or wrong, good or bad, positive or negative, etc. Judgments can be helpful during our daily lives when we want to make effective decisions. But this process needs to be suspended during the time devoted to meditation. If judgments enter our minds without conscious intention, we observe the judgments themselves with bare attention. We must be careful not to fall into the trap of judging our judgments!

Bare of decision means not trying to determine any future courses of action while we are meditating. Even if waves of creative ideas cross our minds during meditation, we resist the temptation to dwell on them. We just continue to observe our experiences as they arise from moment to moment.

Bare of mental commentary means examining the mind without engaging in an internal dialogue. The mind has an opinion on everything! Sometimes we get hooked into the mind's comments because we believe the mind has something profound to say. It never does!

An insight, which *is* profound, is not a thought. An insight is a nonconceptual realization of the way things really are. We can think about an insight after it occurs, but we cannot think our way into an insight. During the time devoted to meditation, just mindfully observe what is present. In this way insights will naturally arise on their own.

MOMENTARY CONCENTRATION

We all have the ability to concentrate, to focus our minds. However, it is possible to cultivate varying degrees or levels of concentration. The deepest levels are developed by attending to a single object of awareness (such as the breath), intentionally excluding everything but this object from entering our minds. Every time our minds start to wander, we bring them back to our primary object of attention. When our attention is strong enough, we become "absorbed" in that object and experience profound feelings of bliss and tranquillity. However, this level of concentration is too deep for our current purposes.

During insight meditation we want to gain insight into the true nature of our experience. To accomplish this we need to observe each of our experiences, without excluding any of them, to determine their common characteristics. There is a level of concentration, prior to becoming "absorbed," where the mind has the ability to stay focused on whatever arises within consciousness. This more fluid type of awareness is referred to as *momentary concentration,* since the mind is able to observe whatever it is presented with on a moment-to-moment basis. This type of concentration is conducive to generating insight and is automatically cultivated as we practice insight meditation.

THE TRUE CHARACTERISTICS OF EXPERIENCE

Our experiences in life are impermanent, unsatisfactory, and selfless. Each time we become aware of this, we are observing the true characteristics of our experience. As these characteristics are repeatedly observed, our perceptual distortions (the beliefs directly contrary to an understanding of these characteristics) weaken and are eventually eradicated.

Everything in this world is *impermanent*. Our relationships, bodies, thoughts, and even consciousness itself are in a constant state of flux or change. Yet, we cling to these things as if they will last forever. Observing impermanence means that we directly perceive the incessant rise and fall of every one of our experiences. When, through first-hand observation, the mind becomes convinced of the fact of impermanence, it stops grasping at its experiences and learns to surrender to each new moment.

There are many pleasant experiences in life. Since each experience is impermanent and unable to provide a lasting sense of happiness, however, all experiences are ultimately *unsatisfactory*. The mind that has not realized unsatisfactoriness keeps grasping at each new experience in a futile attempt to discover a permanent source of satisfaction. As we begin to witness this useless struggle, we come to appreciate the suffering that each of us experiences.

As we pay bare attention to our mind and body, we discover that they are in a perpetual state of change. Everything in our experience is constantly becoming other than it was just a moment before. It is not that everything is impermanent, but that impermanence is the only "thing" that there is! If everything is continually changing, nothing—no "thing"—exists for even a moment in time. If this is true, where is the permanent self to which we constantly refer?

Observing selflessness is witnessing how our moment-to-moment experiences arise and pass away without the presence (or necessity) of a permanent self. Life is merely a process which perpetuates itself through certain causes and conditions. (We will explore these causes and conditions at a future point in our journey.)

Selflessness is the most subtle and difficult characteristic to observe. However, when we discover this characteristic for ourselves, we experience a sense of freedom that words cannot describe.

During meditation, you do not have to look for each of these characteristics individually; they are all interrelated. When you realize impermanence, you are also seeing the unsatisfactory and selfless nature of your experience.

We are now ready to complete the basic instructions for the practice of insight meditation. It will become apparent how this meditation process is based upon the application of the three principles we have been discussing: paying bare attention, developing momentary concentration, and observing the true nature of our experience.

As we indicated in our discussion regarding the first two sets of instructions, it may be helpful to record these directions and play them back during your first few meditation sessions. Leave enough time after each statement so that you can practice what you are being instructed to do. The actual instructions take fifteen or twenty minutes, but you can record the sound of a bell at the end of forty-five or sixty minutes to indicate the end of the meditation session. (The original two sets of instructions are repeated before adding the new material.)

INSIGHT MEDITATION INSTRUCTIONS

DEVELOPING AWARENESS OF HABITS

❖ Your eyes are closed.

❖ Your mouth is closed and you are breathing through your nose.

❖ Feel the touch sensation of your breath as it flows in and out of your nostrils at the tip of your nose. Some people feel the sensation more strongly within the nostrils, while others feel it more on the upper lip.

❖ To help you locate where you feel the touch sensation of the breath most distinctly, inhale deeply and force the air out through your nostrils. Wherever you feel the sensation most clearly and precisely is the place to keep your attention focused for the balance of the meditation period.

❖ Feel the beginning, the middle, and the end of every in-breath, and the beginning, the middle, and the end of every out-breath.

❖ Sometimes the breath will be short—there is no need to make it longer. Sometimes the breath will be long—there is no need to make it shorter. Sometimes the breath will be erratic—there is no need to even it out.

❖ Just become aware of the breath as it goes in and out of the nostrils at the tip of the nose.

❖ Feel the beginning, the middle, and the end of every in-breath, and the beginning, the middle, and the end of every out-breath.

❖ Let the breath breathe itself.

❖ Notice how the quality or experience of every in-breath is different from the quality or experience of every out-breath.

❖ Notice how the quality or experience of every in-breath is different from the quality or experience of every other in-breath, and how the quality or experience of every out-breath is different from the quality or experience of every other out-breath.

❖ Notice the impermanent and changing nature of each breath.

❖ As you focus on the breath, notice that from time to time your attention shifts to other experiences or new objects of awareness. *This is not a problem.*

❖ Whenever your attention shifts to an object other than the breath, merely become aware of the impermanent and changing nature of that object. Then, gently but firmly, bring your attention back to the touch sensation of the breath.

❖ For example, while you are following the breath
   you may become aware of a pleasant physical
   sensation in the body. Becoming aware of that
   sensation means that you no longer have your
   attention focused on the breath. Instead of
   berating yourself for not staying with the breath,
   merely observe how that sensation also has a
   beginning, a middle, and an end (i.e., that the
   sensation is impermanent and constantly
   changing). Then, gently but firmly, draw your
   attention back to the breath, your primary object
   of attention, continuing to watch it rise and fall.

❖ If an unpleasant sensation, such as itching,
   tightness, or pain arises, and your attention is
   drawn to that sensation, merely observe its
   beginning, middle, and end. Then, gently but
   firmly, place your attention back on the touch
   sensation of the breath.

❖ If one of your senses is stimulated, and a sense
   impression such as hearing, smelling, tasting, or
   touching arises and takes your attention away
   from the breath, simply observe how that sense
   experience also has a beginning, a middle, and an
   end. Then, gently but firmly, return to the breath,
   watching it rise and fall.

❖ If a pleasant thought or image arises, you may
   experience a tendency to chase after that thought
   or image to see where it will lead and to derive as
   much pleasure from that thought or image as you

possibly can. Instead, when you realize that your attention has been taken away from your breath, merely notice the beginning, the middle, and the end of that pleasant thought or image. See how the thought or image is merely an impermanent process. Then, gently but firmly, place your attention back on the touch sensation of your breath.

❖ If an unpleasant thought or image arises, you may experience a tendency to suppress or push that thought or image out of your mind, so that you do not have to encounter the unpleasant feelings associated with it. Instead, when you become aware that an unpleasant thought or image has arisen, experience the beginning, the middle, and the end of that thought or image. Then, gently but firmly, place your attention back on the touch sensation of the breath.

❖ If the mind begins to judge itself for not staying focused on the breath, for being so restless, for remembering unpleasant experiences, or for any other activities it may engage in, just experience the judgment as another thought. With bare attention become aware of its beginning, middle, and end, and then gently but firmly draw your attention back to your breath.

In conclusion, use your breath both as a centering device to help you develop momentary concentration and as an object that will help you cultivate bare attention (i.e., the nonjudg-mental observation of what is taking place within your mind from moment to moment). You want to be able to directly experience the impermanent nature of your breath. When your attention is drawn to other objects of awareness, such as sensations, sense impressions, thoughts, or images, notice their impermanent nature as well. Then, gently but firmly, go back to following the breath—your primary object of attention.

Please open your journal (Journal Entry 6) and record the thoughts, feelings, images, and insights that arose during this meditation period. You can use the following questions as a way of exploring your experience. There are no right or wrong answers.

❖ What did you learn about your mind?

❖ What obstacles to paying "bare attention" did you encounter?

❖ What were your insights regarding the impermanent nature of your experience?

❖ What were your insights regarding the unsatisfactory nature of your experience?

❖ What were your insights regarding the selfless nature of your experience?

❖ What were the ways in which you began to sense how the three characteristics of impermanence, unsatisfactoriness, and selflessness may all be interrelated?

Journal Entry 6   *Date:* _____

_____

_____

_____

_____

_____

_____

_____

_____

_____

_____

_____

_____

_____

_____

_____

_____

_____

_____

_____

_____

_____

_____

_____

_____

_____

_____

_____

_____

_____

_____

_____

_____

_____

_____

_____

_____

_____

_____

_____

_____

_____

_____

_____

_____

_____

_____

_____

_____

_____

_____

_____

_____

_____

_____

_____

WALKING MEDITATION

In addition to sitting, one can practice a walking form of insight meditation. There are many benefits to this type of practice. For example, if our legs get cramped after sitting for long periods of time, walking meditation provides the opportunity to stretch them.

The greatest value from walking meditation is that it supports the arising of insight. Through walking meditation we are able to see how a psychological act of *intention* precedes each physical movement. We can observe how each action is comprised of many submovements that arise and pass away with incredible speed.

We can also experience how each movement, together with the intention that precedes it, is impermanent and unsatisfactory and occurs without the presence of a self.

Meditators usually alternate between the sitting and walking forms of meditation. The typical sequence is either forty-five minutes of sitting and fifteen minutes of walking, or sixty minutes of sitting and thirty minutes of walking. Please read the following instructions and then practice your first walking meditation session.

WALKING MEDITATION INSTRUCTIONS

To practice walking meditation, find a straight and level walkway which continues for about twenty-five feet. This path length prevents you from having to constantly stop and turn around to continue walking. A longer path would not be suitable, since without the need to stop occasionally, it would be too easy for your mind to drift and lose its concentration.

❖ Each of the following steps are to be performed in *slow motion*. As you walk, cultivate momentary concentration, apply the principles of bare attention, and observe the three characteristics of your experience.

❖ Begin with both feet touching the floor and with your hands at your sides. Stay in this posture for about a minute, until your concentration is centered on the rise and fall of your breath (see figure 13).

FIGURE 13   FIGURE 14   FIGURE 15

❖ Slowly raise your hands and place the palm of one hand on your abdomen and the palm of the other hand on top of the first. (Which hand is placed on top does not matter.) Look down at the ground at a point about three feet in front of you (see figure 14).

❖ Your mouth is closed and you are breathing through your nose. You are going to coordinate the stages of the walking process with your breath.

❖ Begin by slowly raising the heel of your right foot and coordinating this movement with your inhalation.

❖ After lifting the right heel (with your toes still touching the ground), maintain this posture and slowly exhale (see figure 15).

FIGURE 16   FIGURE 17   FIGURE 18

❖ As you raise your right foot off the floor and shift it forward, slowly inhale (see figure 16).

❖ Drop your right foot to the floor and slowly exhale at the same time (see figure 17).

❖ As you begin lifting the heel of your left foot, coordinating it with your inhalation, move your body slightly forward to maintain your balance. After the left heel is lifted (with your toes still touching the ground), maintain this posture and slowly exhale (see figure 18).

❖ As you raise your left foot off the floor and shift it forward (a short distance beyond your right foot), slowly inhale (see figure 19).

❖ Drop your left foot to the floor and slowly exhale at the same time (see figure 20).

FIGURE 19   FIGURE 20   FIGURE 21

❖ As you once again begin lifting the heel of your right foot, coordinating it with your inhalation, move your body slightly forward to maintain your balance (see figure 21).

❖ Continue with the slow walking movements. When you reach the end of the walkway, stop and drop your hands to your sides. Stay in this posture for a short while until your concentration is centered on the rise and fall of your breath.

❖ Raise your hands, placing them on your abdomen as you did before, and begin turning around. Lift the heel of your right foot, raise that foot off the floor, shift it toward the right, and slowly drop it to the floor. Then, lift the heel of your left foot, raise that foot off the floor, shift it toward the right, and slowly drop it to the floor parallel to the right foot. Repeat the sequence of steps until the turn is completed. Coordinate each of your turning movements with your breath as you did when walking straight ahead.

❖ When you complete your turn and are facing the length of the path once again, drop your hands to your sides. Remain in this posture until your concentration is centered on the rise and fall of your breath.

❖ Repeat the entire sequence for the duration of the meditation session.

In summary, the walking process involves four stages: lifting, raising, shifting, and dropping. Your inhalation is coordinated with the lifting movement of the heel of your foot and your exhalation with keeping your foot lifted, while your toes are still touching the ground. Your inhalation is coordinated with the raising and shifting movements and your exhalation with the dropping of your foot. While you are coordinating your breath with your physical movements, remember to pay bare attention to what is taking place; avoid making judgments, decisions, or comments.

Observe the impermanent nature of your walking experience: the intention that precedes each movement, the movement itself, and every breath which rises and falls from moment-to-moment. When your mind shifts to another object of awareness, focus on seeing that it is also impermanent. Then, gently but firmly, place your attention back on your walking movements, coordinating them with your breath.

Please open your journal (see Journal Entry 7) and record the thoughts, feelings, images, and insights that arose during your first walking meditation session. You can use the following questions as a way of exploring your experience. There are no right or wrong answers.

❖ What did you learn about the interrelatedness of your mind and body?

❖ What body sensations did you experience?

❖ Did those sensations change with each phase of the walking process?

❖ Was it easier to pay bare attention during walking or sitting meditation?

❖ What were your insights regarding impermanence?

❖ What were your insights regarding unsatisfactoriness?

❖ What were your insights regarding selflessness?

❖ What were the ways in which you began to sense how the three characteristics of impermanence, unsatisfactoriness, and selflessness may all be interrelated?

❖ In what way is the person who started the walking meditation different from the person who finished?

Journal Entry 7   *Date:* _____

_____

_____

_____

_____

_____

_____

_____

_____

_____

_____

_____

_____

_____

_____

_____

_____

_____

_____

_____

_____

_____

_____

_____

_____

_____

CLEAR COMPREHENSION

Unless one is on a retreat or living the life of a recluse, practicing the sitting and walking forms of meditation takes only a short amount of time each day. To reach the center of our being, we need to orient our entire lives toward that goal. Clear comprehension, which has its roots in Buddhist psychology, is a psychological process that enables us to extend our awareness into the active or engaged part of our lives. By extending our awareness in this manner, we transform every moment into an opportunity for gaining self-mastery. There are four types of clear comprehension: clearly understanding our intentions, clearly understanding appropriateness, clearly understanding the scope of meditation, and clearly understanding our true nature.

Clearly understanding our intentions means becoming clear about the purpose of the activities we engage in throughout the day, making sure that we participate only in those activities that support our inward journey. To develop this type of clear comprehension, we need to pause before beginning each new activity to determine whether our intended thoughts, words, or deeds will take us closer to or further from our goal.

If we discover that an intention to think, speak, or act in a particular way is motivated by greed, hatred, or a general state of confusion, we would merely allow the intention to rise and fall within the mind without acting upon it. If, on the other hand, we discover that an intention is motivated by generosity, lovingkindness, or wisdom, we would encourage ourselves to pursue that behavior.

It is the process of paying bare attention that gives us the psychological space to consider the initial intentions behind our behaviors before a layer of secondary justifications and rationalizations arises. Without paying bare attention to our initial motivations, our secondary considerations might lead us to engage in activities that will produce an undesirable result.

The following examples illustrate how clearly understanding our intentions works:

❖ If you are about to touch someone, you would stop and observe (with bare attention) your intention to touch the other person. If you discover that the intention of the touch is to subtly intimidate, you would allow the intention to pass away without acting upon it. However, if the intention is to express compassion or support, you would allow the action to occur.

❖ If you are about to offer an individual some advice, you would stop and observe (with bare attention) your intention to offer the advice. If you discover that the intention of the advice is to manipulate the other person, you would allow the intention to pass away without acting upon it. However, if the intention is to help the person avoid experiencing some difficulties, you would allow yourself to communicate the advice.

❖ If thoughts about the future come to mind, you would stop and observe (with bare attention) your intention to think about the future. If you discover that your intention to think about the future is to avoid dealing with a current issue, you would allow the intention to pass away without acting upon it. However, if the intention is to think through the most effective way of handling

a current issue, you would allow this line of
thinking to occur.

Clearly understanding appropriateness means becoming clear about
the suitability of an intended action. Although an action may
be aligned with our goals and based upon wholesome intentions, we still need to consider whether our intended words,
thoughts, or deeds are in harmony with the current set of circumstances. If we ignore considerations of time and place and
attempt to superimpose our agenda over any situational limitations, we set ourselves up for frustration and failure.

The following examples illustrate how clearly understanding appropriateness works:

❖ If someone is communicating with you a recent
    loss and you determine that your intention to
    touch that person is motivated by compassion,
    you still need to decide whether that touch is
    likely to be misinterpreted by the recipient. For
    example, if the person you are about to touch is a
    member of the opposite sex, you have to consider
    whether the touch could be misconstrued as a
    sexual advance. If this is the case, you would
    refrain from physically touching that person and
    express your compassion in more suitable ways.

❖ If one of your friends is telling you about a
    problem he or she is having and you determine
    that your intention to give advice is motivated by
    the desire to be helpful, you still need to consider
    if your friend is merely using the communication
    as an opportunity to vent his or her frustration or

anger, rather than wanting to hear any advice at this time. If this is the case, you would withhold your advice and continue to listen.

❖ If you decide that your intention to think about the future is motivated by a desire to bring an aspect of your life into alignment with your goal of achieving self-mastery, you still need to consider whether you have enough information to assure that this reflection will be a worthwhile investment of your time. Although there may be some value in considering alternatives, a better use of your time may be to collect additional information about your choices.

Clearly understanding the scope of meditation means becoming clear about the domain, range, or extent of our meditation practice. In this context our "practice" encompasses more than the sitting and walking forms of meditation. It means approaching each moment of our lives with the question, "How can I use this present moment to further my awakening process?"

Unless there is a specific intention to penetrate each and every aspect of our lives with the light of awareness, there are areas of our lives that will remain in darkness even after years of practicing the traditional forms of meditation. We tend to use these "dark" areas as hiding places when we want to avoid dealing with our issues or when we are looking for ways to escape from our everyday problems. Activities used to escape, such as watching television or daydreaming, are not inherently wrong or bad. However, when they are used unskillfully, they act as impediments to achieving self-mastery.

By creating the habit of determining how we can use each

moment of our lives to further our awakening process, we may decide, for example, to continue watching television but to avoid watching programs that foster thoughts of violence. We may choose to continue daydreaming but to change the content of our daydreams from sexual fantasies to thoughts of expressing lovingkindness in the world.

Clearly understanding the scope of meditation helps to build a momentum in our practice of meditation. As we penetrate the hidden parts of our lives with the light of awareness, our actions become more skillful and our minds tend to quiet down. As our minds become calmer, our meditation sessions yield more insights. These insights, in turn, help to transform the active parts of our lives.

Clearly understanding our true nature means becoming clear (i.e., without delusion) about the true nature of our moment-to-moment experience. Of all our perceptual distortions, the most difficult to eradicate is the view or belief that there is a permanent self. In order to clearly understand our true nature, we must specifically focus on eliminating this deep-seated misconception and replace it with the realization of selflessness.

If at this stage of our journey we are trying to realize selflessness, why did we spend so much time learning about our self-image? In an earlier discussion, we pointed to a break in the continuum of mental health prior to the point of enlightenment. This break exists because the attainment of enlightenment requires a synaptic jump to a transcendent level of awareness. Developing a healthy self-image allows us to move along the mental health continuum up to the point where this break occurs. Recognizing selflessness—that we are not the images we have been creating and identifying with—is the synaptic jump that must be taken.

Of course, each of us has a body with varying physical

characteristics and a mind which is aware or conscious of its sensations, perceptions, thoughts, and intentions. However, there is no self to be found inside or outside of this body or mind. To cultivate the clear understanding of our true nature, we need to investigate deeply how our mind and body can operate without the existence of a permanent self.

There is a powerful two-step technique that can help us conduct this investigation. However, it takes the kind of attention and concentration that is cultivated through our meditation practice for this technique to become more than an interesting intellectual exercise.

First, ask yourself before and while engaging in each of your activities, "*Who...?*" For example: Who is walking? Who is eating? Who is angry? Next, examine these experiences to see how they occur without the presence of a self. The following are examples of how this process works:

❖ You realize that you intend to eat. You stop and ask yourself, "Who intends to eat?" You immediately observe your mind, paying bare attention, and discover that the thought, "It is time to eat," arose because your mind became aware of the physical sensation of hunger. In other words, the intention to eat was conditioned by feelings of hunger. There was no independent self that made an isolated or arbitrary decision to eat. The thought occurred because of the interaction between various elements of the mind and body.

❖ As you begin eating, you stop and ask yourself, "Who is eating?" You observe your experience and notice that eating involves both mental intentions (e.g., to look at the food, to pick up a fork, to open the mouth) and the carrying out of those intentions by the body (e.g., the food is looked at, the fork is picked up, the mouth is opened, and so forth). In other words, the physical steps involved in the process of eating are conditioned by the intentions that precede them. There is no independent self in the body that is able to look at the food, pick up the fork, or open the mouth. The body gets its directions from the mind.

❖ As you begin enjoying the food, you stop and ask yourself, "Who is enjoying?" You investigate and realize that, as the food touches the tongue, an agreeable taste is experienced, and this causes a pleasant feeling to enter the mind. In other words, the pleasant feeling was conditioned by the tongue coming into contact with an agreeable taste. The pleasant feeling and the awareness of the pleasant feeling certainly exist, but there is no independent self that is doing the enjoying.

❖ After you finish your meal, your children begin to argue. Your requests for them to stop go unheeded, and you feel anger beginning to arise. At that point you stop and ask yourself, "Who is angry?" You look within your mind and discover thoughts such as, "Why must they always argue? Why can't I just relax after my meal without having to deal with this? Won't they ever learn? What's wrong with them?" You also notice that your body is tense, your breath is quick, and your

face feels warm. You become aware of the
intention to yell at your children and to punish
them for their behavior. In other words, anger is
nothing more than the mind reacting in a
conditioned way to those stimuli which it
perceives as unpleasant. The response of the body
immediately follows the reaction of the mind.
There is no independent self that is angry behind,
beyond, or within the mind-body process. It is
our identification with the thoughts, perceptions,
sensations, or bodily reactions which creates the
illusion that I am angry.

In each case, we can see how one experience conditions the
arising of the next. When the specific condition that caused
the subsequent experience is no longer present, then the result-
ing experience no longer occurs.

In actuality, there are always many causes contributing to
each effect; each effect, in turn, becomes one of many causes.
This *dependent origination* process continues in a never-ending cycle
without the existence, or necessity, of a permanent self.

As we begin to perceive selflessness and stop grasping at
each of our experiences in an attempt to make them permanent, the mind stops struggling and begins to relax. We begin
to realize a contentedness and inner freedom that defies
description.

We will revisit this discussion on selflessness later in our
journey. The following exercise will enable you to begin the
process of clearly understanding our true nature.

EXERCISE: CULTIVATING CLEAR COMPREHENSION

Please *directly examine* your experience and answer the following questions:

Who is answering this question?

Who is comprehending the meaning of this sentence?

Who is trying to transform his or her awareness?

Please open your journal (Journal Entry 8) and record the thoughts, feelings, images, and insights that arose during your experience with clearly understanding your true nature. You can use the following questions as a way of exploring your experience. There are no right or wrong answers.

❖ What difficulties did you encounter while investigating the selfless nature of your experience?

❖ What do you believe is the source of those difficulties?

❖ What did you come to understand about the interaction or interrelatedness of your mind and body?

❖ What did you discover about the selfless nature of your experience?

❖ Who made those discoveries?

Journal Entry 8   *Date:* _____

As we have repeated several times during this phase of our journey, "taming the ox" requires that we transform all aspects of our lives into opportunities to achieve self-mastery. This transformation is accomplished by combining the formal practice of insight meditation with the application of clear comprehension to our moment-to-moment experiences. Our lives must become one with our practice and our practice must become one with our lives.

The next stage of our journey is called "Riding the Ox Home." At this stage we begin to experience the profound peace, freedom, and joy that result from having tamed the ox. Fortunately, the ox does not have to be thoroughly tamed in order for you to begin riding him home!

CHAPTER SIX

RIDING THE OX HOME

INSIGHTS: HERE AND NOW

As we consistently observe our minds through the practice of insight meditation and clear comprehension, we come to realize that all of our thoughts use the concepts of *time* and *space* as reference points. In other words, we discover that our thoughts refer to what has occurred in the past, to what may happen in the future, or to what we believe to be true about the present. By identifying with the content of our thoughts, therefore, we live in a conceptual world of "where" and "when." This is problematic, since the direct experience of life is nonconceptual, and takes place in the "here and now."

To "ride the ox home" we have to learn to be present during each moment of our lives. We continue to use the notions of time and space, but we no longer try to live within the conceptual world that these ideas create.

OBSTACLES: KNOWLEDGE VERSUS KNOWING

The most significant obstacle to living in the moment is that we, as a culture, overvalue the importance of the intellect. From the time we were children, we were taught the value of intellectual prowess. We have been led to believe that we can solve any problem to which we put our minds. While this may be true in the material world, it is certainly not true regarding spiritual matters. In other words, the greatest barrier to reaching our center is believing that the mind can think its way into that experience.

It is crucial to distinguish between a thought and an insight. A thought is a concept or belief that can approximate reality, but is never the same as the reality to which it points. Thoughts are associated with knowledge, which always involves our memories from the past. Thus, if we are tied to our thoughts, we are unable to examine things as they are in the here and now.

An insight, on the other hand, is a direct experience of the reality that exists beyond our concepts and beliefs. Insights are associated with knowing, as opposed to knowledge, because they are grounded in the present moment in reality itself. Insights reveal the true nature of our experience.

Certainly it is important to honor the conceptual mind. We need to use it to learn from the past and to create the type of life we desire in the future. In fact, without the mind's goal of achieving self-mastery, we would not have been able to come this far in our journey. However, our thoughts are not the ultimate passports to the center of our being.

PATH: LIVING IN THE MOMENT

Just how much have we been influenced and controlled by our concepts of time and space? The next two exercises and the discussions that follow will help us answer this question.

EXERCISE: EXPOSING ILLUSIONS ABOUT TIME

Please consider the following questions and answer them by indicating whether they refer to the past, future, or now.

At this moment, what time is it?

When you woke up this morning, what time was it then?

When you go to sleep tonight, what time will it be then?

When you were born, what time was it then?

When you die, what time will it be then?

The answer to each question is "now." It is *always* now! Time exists only in the mind as a relative concept, but we tend to live our lives as if time were an absolute reality.

There is an old story about two monks walking to a monastery during a rainstorm. They rounded a curve and came upon a woman who was standing next to a huge mud puddle, wondering how to get to the other side. The elder monk noticed the woman's dilemma and said to her, "Come, let me help you get across." He picked up the woman, walked through the mud puddle, and put her down on the other side. The two monks then continued their journey to the monastery.

After several hours had passed, the younger monk said to the elder, "I cannot contain myself any longer. You know that as monks we are not supposed to look at women, let alone touch them. Why did you pick her up?" The elder replied, "I put her down on the other side of the mud puddle. You are the one who is still carrying her around!"

The past is nothing but thoughts and images that we keep replaying in the mind; how else could the past be experienced? How much of the past are *you* still carrying around in your mind, preventing you from living in the moment?

And what of the future? Our minds are so future-oriented that the moment we are about to achieve our aspirations, we immediately formulate a new set of goals. Our minds keep playing the "when" game: "I will be happy when I meet someone I love; I will be happy when I get married; I will be happy when I have children; I will be happy when I get divorced." Whatever we have, do, or become never seems to be enough!

How do you wash your dishes? Do you wash your dishes thinking about what you will be doing after you have finished, or are you present in the experience of washing your dishes? In other words, are you living in some imagined future as you complete your task? How do you drive your car? Do you drive your car so you can get someplace else, or are you present in the experience of driving your car? If we are always doing something so that we can move on to the next imagined task, we never feel a sense of satisfaction in our lives.

The future is nothing but thoughts and images that we keep replaying in the mind; how else could the future be experienced? How much of the future are *you* carrying around in your mind, preventing you from living in the moment?

Even "now" is just another concept. In order for there to be a "now," there must be a time when everything stops for at least a moment. However, as we have seen for ourselves, the only constant is change. When we are truly in the moment, there is no past, future, or now. There is only the moment-to-moment flow of life, experienced as if we were peacefully standing on a bridge, watching the incessant movement of water below us. This equanimity can be experienced whether we are sitting still or engaging in vigorous activity.

EXERCISE: EXPOSING ILLUSIONS ABOUT SPACE

Please consider the following questions and answer them by indicating whether they refer to "here" or "there."

Where are you right now?

If you were in England at this very moment, where would you be?

If you were in Asia at this very moment, where would you be?

If you were in the furthest reaches of outer space at this very moment, where would you be?

The answer for each question is "here." You are *always* here. So often we think about how wonderful it will be when we get to another place. (The entire travel industry depends upon it!) The difficulty is that, when we get "there," we are still here!

Even "here" is just another concept. In order for there to *be* a "here," there needs to be a place that stays exactly as it has always been. As we have seen, this condition does not exist.

Time and space, of course, are critical concepts to master. If our life is solely defined and circumscribed by these concepts, however, we are unable to live a fulfilled and rewarding existence. The infinite joys of life are experienced as we learn to live in the present.

A man was walking through a forest when he saw a tiger about to leap at him. He ran as fast as he could, but he had to stop when he came to a cliff. He grasped a vine and jumped over the edge of the cliff, where he hung precariously. Above him was a tiger—instant death. Below him was a thousand-foot drop—instant death. As if that were not enough, a mouse came along and started nibbling at the vine. The man looked around, spotted a strawberry and plucked it. How sweet it tasted!

This story illustrates what it is like to live in the moment. We can do nothing about the past (the tigers that keep chasing us), we can do nothing about the future (the unexpected precipices that await us), and we have little power over the threats to our perceived security (the mice that eat away at our vines). However, by remaining present in each new moment as it unfolds, we are able to live without anxiety or fear. Each moment of our lives becomes a sweet gift, like the strawberry in the story.

For most of us, says one insight meditation teacher, the experience of life is like jumping out of an airplane without a parachute. We grasp at our memories of the past or at our thoughts regarding the future in a desperate attempt to stop ourselves from falling through life. For individuals who live in the moment, however, although the experience of life is still like jumping out of an airplane without a parachute, there is the realization that there is no ground to hit. They just relax into each new moment as it unfolds.

If we look closely at the picture of "riding the ox home," we notice that the person astride the ox is playing a flute. As with the flute player, only when we learn to live in the moment will we really be able to hear and appreciate the beautiful music of life.

The following three exercises will help you learn to live in the moment. After reading the instructions, please start practicing them *now*.

EXERCISE: EXPANDING MINDFULNESS

1. Cut out 100 small pieces of paper (approximately 1″ square) and write "Be Mindful" on each one of them. Hide these notes all around your house, your car, your office, and so on. Every time you find one of these notes, stop what you have been doing and take a moment to bring your awareness to the here and now.

2. Each day set aside a time to slow down your pace while engaged in a particular activity (e.g., washing, dressing, or eating). Work on being more present during each phase of that activity. While washing, for example, observe the intentions that precede each step of the washing process, examine the feeling of having water touch your face, and discover how often your mind drifts into the past or future. This is an excellent exercise to do in conjunction with clearly understanding our true nature.

3. Observe other people to see how much of the time they appear to be running on automatic. Although we cannot read their minds, we can usually sense when individuals are caught up in their thoughts and are not in the moment. The observation needs to be made with bare attention (i.e., without judging the other person). The realization of how little of the time others are in the here and now acts as a wake-up call for ourselves.

Please open your journal (Journal Entry 9) and record the thoughts, feelings, images, and insights that arose during our discussion of learning to live in the moment. You can use the following questions as a way of exploring your experience. There are no right or wrong answers.

❖ How much of your life do you spend dwelling on the past or the future?

❖ How much of your life do you spend looking forward to being somewhere else?

❖ Why is the experience of living in the moment so difficult to achieve?

❖ Why is living in the moment so liberating?

❖ What do you realize now that you had not realized until this point in your journey?

❖ Which exercises are you committed to practicing in order to learn to live more fully in the moment?

Journal Entry 9   *Date:* _____

_____

_____

_____

_____

_____

_____

_____

_____

_____

_____

_____

_____

_____

_____

_____

_____

_____

_____

_____

_____

_____

_____

_____

_____

_____

_____

_____

_____

_____

_____

CHAPTER SEVEN

THE OX TRANSCENDED

INSIGHTS: CAUSE AND EFFECT

We have been using the metaphor of an ox to represent the mind that needs to be tamed. After taming the mind, however, we no longer need the dualistic belief that there is a mind to be tamed and someone who is in the process of taming it. "Transcending the ox" means moving beyond all forms of dualistic thinking and understanding the central principle that governs the mind and, ultimately, every aspect of our lives. This principle is the law of *cause and effect.*

Through our practice of meditation we discover that all things exist as patterns of energy, which are in constant states of motion. Our thoughts or intentions are nothing more than subtle forms of this same energy. The energy created by our thoughts or intentions is never destroyed; it only changes form. Our intention to move, for example, manifests itself as walking, our intention to communicate as speaking, and our intention to think as problem solving.

All things are interrelated and interdependent; nothing exists in isolation. The entire universe is one ecosystem, similar to a spider web—if one part is touched, the entire net shimmers. As a result of interrelatedness and interdependency, every expression of energy, including our thoughts and intentions, ultimately touches and affects everything else.

Expressions of energy that vibrate at the same frequency naturally attract each other. (We express this principle when we say that birds of a feather flock together.) When we create intentions and hold them in mind, these intentions (which interface with everything else in the universe) attract circumstances that produce results that correspond to the nature and quality of those intentions. In other words, we reap in our lives whatever we sow in our minds. When we realize how unfailing this law is and begin to focus our attention on causation, our anxiety about producing results completely disappears.

OBSTACLES: SLOW PROGRESS

We must put the law of cause and effect to the test in order to determine its truth for ourselves. By focusing our intentions on the attainment of self-mastery, we should be able to make swift and visible progress, creating circumstances that fully support our inward journey.

We may find, however, that this is not the case. Our progress may be slow and our circumstances may continue to be uncongenial. This does not mean that the law of cause and effect is not in operation. One reason for the lack of immediate results might be that we are still experiencing the consequences of unskillful (self-destructive) intentions from our past.

In addition, if we have unresolved issues, unskillful thoughts and intentions will continue to enter our minds. If we entertain these thoughts and intentions, which are at cross purposes with our goal of achieving self-mastery, we sabotage our very efforts to achieve that goal. The law of cause and effect is still at work; conflicting causes simply create conflicting effects.

We must continue to apply the law of cause and effect until we root out every self-destructive thought and intention. Only then will we be prepared to comment on the truth and efficacy of this law. The main obstacle to eliminating these self-destructive mindsets is not knowing the right kind of effort to apply.

PATH: RIGHT EFFORT

Although we need to make an effort to achieve any goal, the effort we make is typically case-specific. The consistency and scope of our effort is directly related to the goal we are trying to achieve and the obstacles we face in its achievement. For the goal of reaching our center, our effort must be undeviating and must encompass every aspect of our inner life. As described in Buddhist psychology, there are four types of right effort:

1. The effort to prevent any unskillful states from entering our minds.

2. The effort to eliminate, as quickly as possible, any unskillful states that may have arisen.

3. The effort to continuously cultivate skillful states.

4. The effort to maintain skillful states once they have arisen.

PREVENTING UNSKILLFUL STATES FROM ARISING

Whenever we experience a sight, sound, smell, taste, touch, or idea, there is always a sensation or feeling associated with that experience. If our mindfulness is not strong enough, we react by clinging to pleasant feelings, resisting unpleasant feelings, or maintaining a dull indifference toward feelings that are neither distinctly pleasant nor unpleasant. These reactions are unskillful because they are based upon the belief that these feelings are "me," "mine," or "myself," and because they cause us to engage in intentional activities that perpetuate the illusion of a permanent self.

The way to prevent these unskillful states from arising is to stand guard at the doors of our senses. We need to pay bare attention to each sense impression as it occurs. When the sense impression arises along with its corresponding feeling, we are to notice, or discern, the true nature of each experience (that it is impermanent, unsatisfactory, and selfless). By training ourselves in this way, we avoid being led astray by perceptual distortions.

ELIMINATING UNSKILLFUL STATES THAT HAVE ARISEN

Only individuals who are fully enlightened remain mindful at all times. Therefore, we should avoid judging ourselves for having allowed unskillful states to arise. After an unsuccessful attempt to eradicate these states through paying bare attention, there are several alternative methods we can employ to eliminate them.

The first technique is to replace an unwholesome thought with its direct opposite. For example, if a thought rooted in greed arises (e.g., the desire to possess what others have), we can replace it with one based upon generosity. If a thought rooted in hatred arises (e.g., anger or irritation over how we are being treated), we can replace it with one based upon love.

The second method is to counter the attraction of the thought by considering the undesirable consequences of allowing the thought to remain in the mind. For example, we can consider that the result of *worry* is anxiety, stress, and fear; the result of *anger* is loss of control, distorted thinking, and a lack of self-respect.

The third technique is to redirect our attention to a different object of awareness. This is similar to closing our eyes to avoid looking at an unpleasant sight. For example, if we begin obsessing about our past failures, we can turn the mind to a consideration of our future goals.

The fourth technique is to investigate the source of our unskillful thoughts. If we are angry, for example, we can examine the mind to determine the origin of our anger. When we discover that our anger originated from our own perceptions and not from the circumstances we encountered, the anger may begin to dissipate on its own.

Finally, if all else fails, we can attempt to suppress the thought by an act of sheer will. This is the least desirable method since the resistance can create a *persistence* of the very thought we are trying to subdue.

CULTIVATING THE FOUR SKILLFUL STATES

By remaining mindful, we are automatically applying this type of effort. However, there are four skillful or "noble" states of mind that are highly desirable to cultivate. These four states, which enhance the quality of our relationships, are lovingkindness, compassion, sympathetic joy, and equanimity.

Lovingkindness is a state of mind through which one expresses an unconditional love for all living beings. It differs from feelings of affection for a loved one in that it is not limited in its scope. It is the desire that everyone, without exception, experience health, happiness, peace, and success. It is a type of caring that does not seek to possess or control and expects nothing in return.

Lovingkindness can be cultivated by taking time each day to practice the following visualization process. You may want to tape the directions and play them back, giving yourself enough time to complete each step. After a while it is likely that you will have memorized the process and listening to the tape will no longer be necessary.

EXERCISE: DEVELOPING LOVINGKINDNESS

❖ Close your eyes.

❖ When you do this exercise for the first time, it
   may be helpful to remember a time in your life
   when someone gave you unconditional love or
   was extremely kind to you. Recall a particular
   incident when you vividly felt this love or
   kindness. Allow the memory of the feelings
   associated with that experience to emerge. These
   are the kind of feelings that you want to project
   during this exercise.

❖ As the following words are repeated, allow the
   images of the individuals to whom they refer to
   arise naturally within your mind. There is no need
   to intentionally imagine certain people.

❖ "May *I* be well, happy, and peaceful. May no harm
   come to me, may no difficulties come to me, may
   no problems come to me, may I always meet with
   success. May I also have patience, courage,
   understanding, and determination to meet and
   overcome the inevitable difficulties, problems,
   and failures in life.

❖ "May *my parents* be well, happy, and peaceful. May
   no harm come to them, may no difficulties come
   to them, may no problems come to them, may
   they always meet with success. May they also have

patience, courage, understanding, and determination to meet and overcome the inevitable difficulties, problems, and failures in life.

❖ "May *my teachers* be well, happy, and peaceful. May no harm come to them, may no difficulties come to them, may no problems come to them, may they always meet with success. May they also have patience, courage, understanding, and determination to meet and overcome the inevitable difficulties, problems, and failures in life.

❖ "May *my relatives* be well, happy, and peaceful. May no harm come to them, may no difficulties come to them, may no problems come to them, may they always meet with success. May they also have patience, courage, understanding, and determination to meet and overcome the inevitable difficulties, problems, and failures in life.

❖ "May *my friends* be well, happy, and peaceful. May no harm come to them, may no difficulties come to them, may no problems come to them, may they always meet with success. May they also have patience, courage, understanding, and determination to meet and overcome the inevitable difficulties, problems, and failures in life.

❖ "May *all persons toward whom I feel indifferent* be well, happy, and peaceful. May no harm come to them, may no difficulties come to them, may no problems come to them, may they always meet

with success. May they also have patience,
courage, understanding, and determination to
meet and overcome the inevitable difficulties,
problems, and failures in life.

❖ "May *my enemies* be well, happy, and peaceful. May
no harm come to them, may no difficulties come
to them, may no problems come to them, may
they always meet with success. May they also have
patience, courage, understanding, and
determination to meet and overcome the
inevitable difficulties, problems, and failures in life.

❖ "May *all living beings* be well, happy, and peaceful.
May no harm come to them, may no difficulties
come to them, may no problems come to them,
may they always meet with success. May they also
have patience, courage, understanding, and determination to meet and overcome the inevitable
difficulties, problems, and failures in life."

Compassion is the quality of mind that wishes others to be free from suffering. A compassionate individual may realize that each person experiences the results of his or her prior thoughts and intentions, but he or she is willing to be open to the pain and sorrow of others without judgment. By considering the forms of suffering that humans experience (starvation, poverty, sickness, not getting what we want, and losing what we have), our compassion grows. While pity looks down on a person in pain as if to say "poor you," compassion sends the message that we are all in this together. Finally, compassion is the willingness to help others awake to the deeper realities of life without expecting anything in return.

Compassion can also be intentionally cultivated. The next time you encounter someone who is suffering and you are at a loss as to how to help, imagine that you are going through the same pain. Ask yourself, "How would I feel if this were me, and how would I want others to treat me? What would I be wanting most from the people in my life?" Trust your inner response and follow through with the ideas that emerge. Keep aware of how the individual is responding to your efforts so that you can modify them as needed.

Sympathetic joy is a state of mind that rejoices over the prosperity, happiness, and success of others as if they were one's own achievements. It is the antithesis of envy, jealousy, and covetousness. This is a very difficult quality of mind to cultivate, since most of us tend to feel that we are in competition with almost everyone else in the world. When others achieve something that is meaningful to us, we typically feel as though we have lost something as a consequence of their gain.

Sympathetic joy is cultivated by extending the thought "I rejoice in your health, happiness, and success" first to ourselves and then to everyone else, as we did in the exercise for developing lovingkindness. By directing this thought to a specific individual, we can counter any envy or jealousy that arises when we hear of his or her good fortune.

Equanimity is a quality of mind that remains unaffected by the vicissitudes of life. It is not indifference but a type of mental equilibrium. It treats everyone equally, never expressing favoritism or resentment. Equanimity provides a strong foundation for the expression of lovingkindness, compassion, and sympathetic joy.

Equanimity cannot be developed through a rational process in which we attempt to convince ourselves that there is nothing to worry about when we meet with unfortunate circumstances, and nothing to become excited about when we meet with good fortune. Equanimity arises as a result of gaining deep insight into the impermanent nature of all experience. When the mind realizes that nothing in the world can be relied upon for a lasting sense of security, its reactivity automatically ceases. Equanimity is the experience of being in each new moment without grasping or pushing and merely allowing life to express itself through us.

MAINTAINING SKILLFUL STATES

Mindfulness gives us the ability to detect the quality of mind that we are experiencing from moment to moment. Once we discover that a skillful state has arisen, we make the effort to maintain its presence at the forefront of our minds. In this way, our skillful states gradually increase in strength and stability.

As we root out self-destructive qualities of mind and maintain skillful states, we are able to see for ourselves the truth and efficacy of the law of cause and effect. We realize that our current intentions are directly attracting circumstances that are conducive to the attainment of self-mastery. However, knowing that we have the ability to manifest the type of life we choose can become another trap, preventing us from completing our journey. The power to create tends to keep us identified with the role of being a "creator," or with the content of our own "creations." In the next stage of our journey, "Both Ox and Self Transcended," we move beyond all forms of identification and experience the contentment and freedom that comes from a mind unfettered by self-definitions.

Please open your journal (Journal Entry 10) and record the thoughts, feelings, images, and insights that arose during our discussion of right effort. You can use the following questions as a way of exploring your experience. There are no right or wrong answers.

❖ Which experiences in your life have clearly demonstrated how the law of cause and effect operates?

❖ Which feelings do you find yourself identifying with more: your pleasant, unpleasant, or neutral ones? Why do you believe that this identification occurs?

❖ Which techniques for eliminating unskillful states of mind have you successfully used? Which new methods are you committed to trying?

❖ What are the qualities of lovingkindness that distinguish it from the experience of emotional love?

❖ Who in your life has expressed compassion toward you when it was needed the most? How did they manifest that compassion?

❖ What have been your barriers to expressing sympathetic joy toward people outside your circle of family members and friends?

❖ What do you believe are the positive consequences of cultivating equanimity?

Journal Entry 10   *Date:* _____

CHAPTER EIGHT

BOTH OX AND SELF TRANSCENDED

INSIGHTS: SELFLESSNESS

Because the many roles we play and the many thoughts we think all appear to validate the existence of a personal self, freeing ourselves from the prison of self-identification seems an impossible task. But freeing ourselves is not only possible, it is the very process that comprises this next stage of our journey. The picture that corresponds to this stage, "Both Ox and Self Transcended," is an empty circle that represents the ultimate insight into selflessness.

OBSTACLES: DUALISTIC THINKING

The mind's habitual proclivity to identify with its own concepts or ideas creates obstacles to enlightenment. In dualistic thinking, for example, the mind tends to see things in terms of black and white, and believes that two opposing points of view cannot both be valid. As a consequence, we find ourselves rigidly identifying with one side of an issue or another. This type of polarization keeps us dogmatically tied to our own point of view.

Even if we do not hold rigidly to a particular point of view, however, the natural tendency of the mind to form concepts itself acts as a barrier to seeing the nonconceptual reality that lies beyond the border of our ideas.

Another obstacle frequently encountered at this stage is the fear of losing one's "self" through the process of enlightenment. Since enlightenment cannot be understood conceptually, we feel a sense of vulnerability when we begin to consider what the experience must be like. We fear that if we stop clinging to our bodies, feelings, perceptions, thoughts, and acts of consciousness as though they are our "selves," we will totally disappear. This fear, however, is based upon the mistaken belief that a self, one that is capable of disappearing, exists to begin with.

A man was hanging by his teeth from a branch of a tree leaning over the edge of a cliff. His hands were tied behind him making it impossible for him to free himself. A traveler came upon the man and asked, "Can I help you?"

What a dilemma! If the man opened his mouth to reply, he would fall into the abyss. If he said nothing, the traveler would eventually walk away.

When discussing enlightenment, we experience a similar dilemma. Attempting to use words to describe the experience is like falling into a conceptual abyss. Words can lead to the erroneous conclusion that enlightenment is an experience of something. Remaining silent on the subject could also be misconstrued, leading to the conclusion that enlightenment is an experience of nothing. The difficulty with trying to communicate about enlightenment is that the experience itself is beyond the dualistic concepts of something and nothing, and even beyond the concept of beyond!

PATH: MOVING BEYOND MIND TRAPS

Each of these obstacles can be overcome. To free ourselves from the trap of dualistic thinking, we need to see how opposing points of view can both be valid. The following story illustrates this point.

There was a marriage counselor who saw patients in his home. One day the counselor's wife was in the room next to his office and inadvertently overheard what was taking place during two counseling sessions.

A woman who came for therapy told the counselor that her husband was the source of all the problems in her family. Every time the woman called her husband at work, she was told that he wasn't there. He came home late each night and would never tell her where he had been. When he finally did come home, he would yell at the children for no apparent reason. After hearing her story, the counselor told the woman, "You are right! Your husband is the source of the problems in your family." The woman thanked the counselor and left.

A few minutes later, the woman's husband came to tell the counselor his side of the story. He was not at work when his wife called because he had been fired as a result of his wife's frequent calls. He came home late at night because he had started a new job, which he hadn't told his wife about because he was afraid of being fired again. He was not yelling at the children when he came home, but warning them to watch out, since his wife had a habit of throwing things. After hearing his story the counselor told the man, "You are right! Your wife is the source of the problems in your family." The man thanked the counselor and went home.

After the clients left, the counselor's wife came into her husband's office to speak to him. "I am very confused," she began.

"After listening to the wife's story, you told her that *she* was right. Then, after listening to the husband's version, you told him that *he* was right. I do not believe that they can *both* be right, so which one is?" The counselor looked at his wife and simply replied, "You are!"

To break our attachment to dualistic thinking, we have to begin by realizing that everyone is right from his or her own point of view. In other words, each point of view is relatively true.

In addition to right versus wrong, point of view applies to other dichotomies, such as good versus bad, valuable versus worthless, important versus unimportant, and so forth. As a brief exercise, try to name something that *everyone* considers to be important.

No matter what object or situation you think of, there will always be someone who thinks that the object or situation is unimportant. Is money important? Not to a monk. Is life important? Not to someone who wants to die. It is the same for all opposing concepts; you can always find people who are identified with one point of view or the other. It is only due to the magic show that takes place in our minds that one point of view seems to be inherently true to us.

There is, however, an important distinction to be made concerning the skillfulness of various points of view. Although there is no point of view that is ultimately "right," points of view are either skillful or unskillful depending on whether they lead us closer to or further from our goals. Some points of view, for example, can lead to behaviors that are contrary to those which support our quest for enlightenment. As we discussed in the section on clear comprehension, we need to avoid engaging in behaviors that are rooted in a point of view that reflects greed, hatred, or delusion. On the other hand, we should encourage behaviors that are based upon points of view that reflect generosity, lovingkindness, compassion, and wisdom.

Although skillful points of view lead to circumstances conducive to the experience of enlightenment, attachment to our points of view, or to concepts in general, presents a formidable barrier to realizing the nonconceptual nature of reality. Our point of view may correspond to reality, but it is never the same as the reality to which it points. When we identify with any point of view, we are stuck within a prison created by our own minds, as the following riddle illustrates.

A goose, wedged upside down in a bottle, is dying of suffocation and must be saved. However, the bottle is quite valuable and cannot be broken or modified in any way. How will you get the goose out of the bottle? (Decide on what you would do before reading any further.)

Some people have suggested that we try pulling the goose out by its tail feathers. Others have proposed that we grease the neck of the bottle and try sliding it out, that we pour water inside the bottle and try floating it out, or that we place another goose outside the bottle to motivate the goose to come out on its own. None of these suggestions will work, however, since the goose is too tightly wedged in the bottle. How then do we liberate the goose?

Give up?

The answer is, "The goose is already out of the bottle!" You see, most people never ask how the goose got into the bottle. Our mind automatically looks at the situation in terms of the duality with which it was presented; that is, the physical goose is either in or out of the bottle. The way to solve this riddle is to look at both sides of the duality and accept neither! The goose is in the bottle only by virtue of a mental construct which said that it was in there. If we do not get trapped within the "conceptual bottle" that this riddle intentionally created, all we have to do to liberate the goose (i.e., our minds) is to move beyond our dualistic thinking and see things as they really are.

In fact, every time we feel as if we are trapped in some kind of bottle (i.e., when we have a problem), it is because we are identifying with a particular point of view regarding our current circumstance, as if that point of view were an absolute reality. To further illustrate this point, please complete the following exercise.

EXERCISE: EXAMINING PROBLEMS

List three problems with which you are currently dealing.

1. _____

2. _____

3. _____

Clearly identify your points of view regarding each of these problems (e.g., that you are being treated unfairly, that you have lost something significant, that someone else is wrong, that you do not have something you need, or that the situation is terrible).

1. _____

2. _____

3. _____

Record what you believe to be the opposing point of view that someone else could maintain (e.g., that you are being treated fairly, that what you lost was insignificant, that someone else was right, that you do not need what you do not have, or that there are advantages to being in this situation).

1. _____

2. _____

3. _____

Consider each problem and ask yourself, "If I stopped identifying with my position regarding each problem and took the
opposing point of view, would I still have a problem?"

1. _____

2. _____

3. _____

Would you still have a problem? The answer is a resounding *no*! I am not suggesting, however, that you should adopt the opposing point of view. I am merely illustrating that problems are created when we identify with *any* mental construct. Achieving this broader perspective takes much practice and patience to master, since the imagined self clings to positions and concepts in an attempt to assert or validate itself. By continuing to train the mind, we break through the barriers presented by our conceptual thinking and prepare ourselves for the experience of enlightenment.

To overcome the fear of losing one's self and disappearing into some imagined void, we do not have to convince ourselves that the self does not actually exist. As a consequence of practicing insight meditation and applying clear comprehension to our moment-to-moment experience, we automatically gain insight into the impermanent and selfless nature of our mind and body. As we begin to see things without rigidly identifying with them, the fear starts to dissipate on its own.

It is helpful, nonetheless, to explore the specific ways in which we define ourselves. We need to determine whether any of our self-definitions are absolute realities or are only points of view on a relative continuum. The next exercise will help clarify this idea.

EXERCISE: EXPLORING SELF-DEFINITIONS

Please record the ways in which you have defined yourself over the years. It is important to record as many as you possibly can (short, handsome, strong, funny, interesting, loving, intense, spiritual, generous, disabled, sick, a human, a parent, a child, a teacher, a provider, and so on).

_____   _____   _____

_____   _____   _____

_____   _____   _____

_____   _____   _____

_____   _____   _____

_____   _____   _____

_____   _____   _____

_____   _____   _____

_____   _____   _____

_____   _____   _____

_____   _____   _____

_____   _____   _____

_____   _____   _____

_____   _____   _____

_____   _____   _____

_____   _____   _____

_____   _____   _____

_____   _____   _____

_____   _____   _____

Take the time to thoroughly examine each of your self-definitions. Investigate whether they exist as absolutes or are relative to some other characteristic (e.g., you are short only in relation to others being tall, you are strong only in relation to others being weak, you are spiritual only in relation to others being worldly, or you are disabled only in relation to others being able to do what you cannot).

Every time we define ourselves, we ultimately wind up comparing one concept with another. The reason that we are unable to define what the "self" is (in and of itself) without making conceptual comparisons is that *the self does not actually exist as an individual entity.* Further, no aspect of our mind and body is self-subsistent or exists in any objective way.

However, to say that our psychophysical organisms are nonexistent, or that there is no self, is just another conceptual trap. The concepts of self and no-self are two extremes of a continuum and part of the same dualistic thinking process. We merely talk about "selflessness" to help us root out our attachment to self. The experience of enlightenment (as illustrated in figures 1 and 2 at the beginning of the book) transcends the entire dualistic paradigm. The following metaphor may help to illustrate this point.

Imagine the expansiveness of the sky. The sky is not striving to get anywhere, since there is no place that it does not exist. The sky itself is never affected by anything that takes place under it. To the sky, birth and death are just part of the cycle of life. The sky lives in perfect peace; it just is.

Now envision clouds throughout the sky. Imagine that each cloud has its own shape and is trying to obtain what it considers to be important, or what it believes will make it happy. Figure 22 illustrates what some of these clouds would be saying if they could talk.

Consider for a moment what is preventing these clouds from experiencing the freedom of the sky. As you can see, it is their own points of view about what is important and what will make them happy. In other words, the ways in which they define themselves create the barrier to experiencing things as they really are.

FIGURE 22

Now consider what these clouds need to do to directly experience the freedom of the sky. The answer is that they need to stop identifying with their own points of view. As the lines that define each cloud's self-definition are erased (imagine that occurring), the clouds become one with the sky. However, if you asked what that freedom felt like, the clouds would have no point of reference from which to describe their nonconceptual experience.

Similarly, once we stop identifying with our views of "self," we automatically experience the psychological and spiritual freedom which we refer to as enlightenment. At the moment of enlightenment the concept of an experiencer who is having an experience totally dissolves. It is analogous to what would happen to a salt doll who jumped into the ocean to see what it was like; the doll would become one with the ocean that it was experiencing. As we have been saying, there are no words that can adequately describe the experience of enlightenment.

Please open your journal (Journal Entry 11) and record the thoughts, feelings, images, and insights that arose during this stage of your journey. You can use the following questions as a way of exploring your experience. There are no right or wrong answers.

❖ What are the limitations of dualistic thinking?

❖ What have you discovered about the problems in your life?

❖ Who are you beyond your self-definitions?

Journal Entry 11   *Date:* _____

CHAPTER NINE

REACHING THE SOURCE

INSIGHTS: FREEDOM

What do we find when we "reach the source," when we finally complete the journey to the center? Freedom!

Not a freedom from some *thing*, since nothing has ever existed from which to be free. *It is freedom from the illusion that we are not already free.* When we reach the center of our being, we come to realize, paradoxically, that not a step has been taken. We have journeyed home to a place that we have never left.

Our lives have been plays of consciousness where we have written the scripts, directed the action, played the parts, and watched the performances. Whatever suffering we may have experienced throughout our lives has resulted from identifying with the particular roles that we were playing.

Why and when did these plays of consciousness begin? Each spiritual tradition has a story that metaphorically describes its origin. The following is a Hindu version of how it all began.

Humans once knew of their divine nature. In time, however, they became arrogant and judgmental of the other creatures that walked the face of the earth. The higher gods decided to punish humankind by hiding from them the truth of their own divinity. "Let's hide the truth on top of the highest mountain," suggested one god. "No," replied another, "they will eventually climb that mountain and find it there." "How about hiding it at the bottom of the ocean?" "No," responded another, "some day they will explore the ocean's depths and uncover the truth." "I know what we can do," said the wisest of all the gods, "let's hide the truth deeply within their own minds—*they will never look there!*"

When we do look deeply within our minds and discover our true nature, all psychological and spiritual struggles come to an end. The belief in the existence of a permanent self that needs to compete with all the other selves in the world is eliminated from the deepest strata of our minds. All manifestations of greed and hatred, which were based upon this false view of self, are eradicated. Our words, thoughts, and deeds are perfectly virtuous. Our restless and anxious minds have been tamed. All forms of spiritual blindness have been destroyed, and we see things with perfect understanding. We feel a profound sense of joy, and the course of our lives is observed with an unshakable serenity. We become as natural in our self-expression as are the trees, the birds, and the sky.

OBSTACLES: SUBTLER IDENTIFICATIONS

Completing this stage and reaching the end of our journey is not an easy task; it requires unrelenting effort and a total commitment to the goal. As we continue with our meditation practice and reach deeper levels of awareness, we find that the obstacles become correspondingly more subtle and difficult to detect.

Up until now, we have used cognitive techniques as a way to overcome the obstacles on the path. However, cognitive techniques will only take us so far before they themselves become obstacles to the goal we are trying to achieve. To experience the ultimate in freedom, we need to need to break our identification with the entire cognitive process. As long as the mind grasps at that which is transitory and conditioned, the spiritual freedom that results from a direct experience of the unconditioned cannot be attained.

Another obstacle that may appear at this point is the belief that we have become enlightened. If we consistently practice meditation, it is inevitable that profound experiences will occur. Some of these experiences include the perception of a bright light in our minds; feelings of extreme happiness, bliss, or exhilaration; a deep sense of tranquillity or inner calm; the emergence of confidence in the practice of meditation; vigorous energy; keen perception of the impermanent, unsatisfactory, and selfless nature of phenomena; strong mindfulness; and equanimity.

These experiences are signs that one's meditation is producing positive results. However, these signs can become obstacles when we believe that they are indications that we have completed our journey and achieved enlightenment. This belief is an impediment to making further progress, since we no longer feel the need to keep looking within and discovering the more subtle distortions that still exist within our minds.

As a result of believing that we are enlightened, we may become arrogant, difficult to communicate with, and begin speaking and acting in ways that we assume enlightened beings speak and act (e.g., talking softly, moving slowly, and so on). Arrogance, closed-mindedness, and acting as if enlightened, however, are sure signs that we have not yet arrived at that point.

PATH: ADVANCED INSTRUCTIONS

To remove the more subtle obstacles and beliefs that arise at this stage, it is helpful to work with a skillful teacher. No matter how profound a book may be, it has not been written with our specific needs in mind—we cannot ask a book questions, and a book cannot determine our level of understanding. A teacher can point out the errors in our thinking and suggest forms of meditation that can counter the specific obstacles we are experiencing. The teacher does not have to be fully enlightened in order to help us. Someone who is on the same path and has completed more of the journey than we have can be of great benefit. Before choosing someone as a teacher, however, we must spend time with him or her to observe that individual's behavior in a variety of circumstances. We never know someone's true character until we see how he or she deals with temptation and adversity.

There is a more advanced form of insight meditation that allows us to reach the deeper levels of awareness at this stage of our journey. This technique is typically practiced during a retreat, or at other times when the mind is so calm that we no longer need to use the breath as a centering device.

The instructions for practicing this advanced form of insight meditation follow. Some of the original instructions are repeated before the presentation of the new material. Once again, it may be helpful to record these directions and play them back during your first few meditation sessions. Leave enough time after each statement so that you can practice what you are being instructed to do.

INSIGHT MEDITATION INSTRUCTIONS

REMOVING SUBTLE OBSTACLES

❖ Keep your posture straight but relaxed.

❖ Make a commitment not to move for the entire meditation period.

❖ Your eyes are closed.

❖ Your mouth is closed and you are breathing through your nose.

❖ Feel the touch sensation of your breath as it flows in and out of your nostrils at the tip of your nose.

❖ Let the breath breathe itself.

❖ Notice the impermanent and changing nature of each breath.

❖ Whenever your attention shifts to an object other than the breath, simply become aware of the impermanent and changing nature of that object. Then, gently but firmly, draw your attention back to the touch sensation of the breath.

❖ After your mind calms down and you are able to observe, without effort, the rising and falling of whatever becomes the object of your awareness, stop using the breath as your centering device.

❖ Just apply your momentary concentration to each object as it arises, without attempting to do anything but pay bare attention to what is occurring.

❖ At this point in the practice, even if the mind makes a note as to the impermanent, unsatisfactory, or selfless nature of its own experience, allow this comment to pass without grasping or taking an interest in it.

❖ As soon as you realize that your mind has grasped at an experience, simply notice the rising and falling of that realization.

❖ If you find your mind becoming distracted and unable to remain in each present moment, go back to following the breath as a way to re-center yourself.

The key to this advanced form of insight meditation is to let go of all forms of conscious cognitive intention, whether it is to stay with the breath, or note the impermanent nature of each experience. As we develop the capacity to be present in each moment without grasping, sense impressions, bodily sensations, and cognitive processes begin to fly through the mind like a whirlwind. When the mind realizes the speed at which things are changing, and that this process of change is beyond its control, it momentarily lets go of its clinging to the conditioned. As it does so, we have a direct experience of unconditioned reality, the spiritual freedom that has always been ours.

At this stage of our journey our mindfulness becomes more natural. Instead of consciously reminding ourselves to remain mindful, the act of forgetting wakes us up to the realization that we have forgotten. The quality of mind that is present while being mindful is very light, while there is a feeling of density or sluggishness when mindfulness is lacking. As mindfulness becomes a way of life, the heavy feeling associated with being unmindful acts as an automatic wake-up call. As our capacity to remain mindful throughout the day increases, the distinction between meditation and the rest of our life begins to dissipate. In effect, our life becomes our practice and our practice becomes one with our life.

To guard ourselves against an erroneous belief that we have completed our inner journey, we have to concede to ourselves that the possibility of reaching deeper levels of awareness still remains. We also need to watch the ways in which others are responding to us. If the people in our lives are communicating that we have become arrogant or that we are acting as if we have all the answers, we need to evaluate our presumptions about where we are in our inner development.

As we accept that we have more work to do, and as we continue to practice diligently, we are able to break through the more subtle barriers to enlightenment. Our deep understanding enables us to help others who are just beginning their journey or who have not come as far along the path. Helping others, in turn, supports our own inner work. The mutual benefit that comes from teaching is the essential understanding that is gained as we complete the last stage of our journey back "in the world."

Please open your journal (Journal Entry 12) and record the thoughts, feelings, images, and insights that arose during this stage of your journey. You can use the following questions as a way of exploring your experience. There are no right or wrong answers.

❖ Has your life become more natural since beginning the journey to the center? If so, in what way?

❖ What is the difference between the experiences that occur within the mind and the mental process of knowing that those experiences are occurring?

❖ How are the mind and body related?

❖ What evidence can you find for mental conditioning or the habit of "running on automatic"?

❖ What other insights about the true nature of experience have arisen?

❖ What benefits have you realized from practicing insight meditation?

Journal Entry 12   *Date:* _____

CHAPTER TEN

IN THE WORLD

INSIGHTS: LIVING AN ENLIGHTENED LIFE

The quality of our lives will always correspond to whatever level of understanding we have achieved. When we are fully enlightened, every word, thought, and deed is wholesome and skillful, and every interaction is permeated with compassion and unconditional love.

Without judgments, prejudices, or psychic distortions, we provide a safe environment that enables others to grow to their fullest potential. By not grasping on to what was true in the past, we demonstrate how to live in the moment. Since we have seen beyond our own veils of ignorance, we are able to see beyond those of the people we meet. We speak to that place within each person that already knows the truth.

Some individuals who have reached profound levels of understanding may decide to become spiritual guides. They may choose to reside in monasteries, meditation centers, or by themselves in reclusive environments. There they have the opportunity to further their own practice, write about the path to enlightenment, or spend time working directly with students. These spiritual guides have become masters as opposed to teachers. While a teacher teaches from the outside in using knowledge, a master teaches from the inside out using wisdom. In other words, those who have achieved self-mastery know that actual truth can never be taught through words alone. They assist their students in turning within to discover truth as it manifests itself through their own personal experience.

Those who do not teach in a formal sense still significantly touch those with whom they come into contact. Their clarity of mind and openness of heart is reflected in every aspect of their lives. Their speech is gentle, kind, and purposeful. Their forms of livelihood never bring harm to anyone. Their relationships are loving, compassionate, and harmonious. In everything they do, they represent what it means to live an enlightened life.

OBSTACLES: TEACHING THROUGH WORDS

"There are many teachers and very few students." This adage makes the point that it is far easier to teach others than it is to follow our own advice. Teaching is one of the strongest and subtlest traps for our ego or sense of self. We are attracted to the power, adoration, special treatment, and lifestyle that spiritual teachers appear to experience. Those who aspire to be teachers may underestimate the dedication, hard work, and responsibility involved. They may crave the benefits without recognizing the effort needed to achieve them. Most importantly, they may not have reached the level of understanding necessary to guide others in the search for truth.

There was once a monk who studied with a teacher for ten years. He told the teacher that he was ready to leave the monastery to teach. The monk went to a remote village and moved into a hut, but no one came for instruction. The monk then went back to the teacher and continued to practice under his tutelage for another ten years. When he later returned to the same village, people came from miles around to learn from him.

If we try to teach before we are ready to do so, we may soon discover that no one is truly listening. We need to have gained significant insight into our personal lives and into the nature of life itself before we are ready to help others free themselves of their own confusion. A person who is stuck in the mud cannot help another person who is stuck in the mud.

We also need to consider whether we have the capacity for presenting material clearly and according to each student's level of understanding. We must evaluate our intention for teaching to determine whether we are being driven by the desire to gain respect, admiration, or power, as opposed to being motivated by generosity and compassion for the suffering of others.

It is also important to remember that, although we may choose to be teachers, not everyone will choose to be our student. We must learn to look for cues to determine whether people are interested in truly hearing what we have to say.

A fundamental obstacle to living an enlightened life is engaging in relationships, forms of livelihood, and other activities that bring harm to ourselves or others. As we guard our minds against the influence of greed, hatred, and delusion, we inevitably discover that there is a disparity between certain aspects of our lives and our inner understanding. We need to begin the difficult process of making conscious decisions regarding the ways in which we live our lives each day.

PATH: LIVING LIFE AS A TEACHING

If we choose to become teachers, we need not wait until we are perfectly enlightened before beginning to teach. With a theoretical understanding of the path, an open heart, and a degree of true insight, both you and the people you teach will benefit greatly.

There is a story by René Daumal entitled *Mount Analogue*. It is the tale of a man who searches for a mountain that few have found and fewer still have climbed. In this story, the man arranges an expedition to find the mountain and eventually arrives at its base with the rest of his team. As the hikers climb toward the summit, they encounter nothing but tundra. Day after day, there is only ice and snow extending for miles. After several days of climbing in this vast wilderness of open and desolate space, they see a small cabin with smoke coming out of its chimney.

As they enter the shelter, they discover a feast spread out on a table, but the people who prepared this meal are nowhere to be found. The climbers glance quizzically at their guide, who tells them to look out the window. When they do, they see another group of hikers waving at them as they climb further up the mountain. "You see," says the guide, "there is an unwritten law in the mountains. It states that you cannot climb higher unless you are willing to support the people who are on the way to the heights you have already reached."

Teaching is a wonderful way of being in the world. By opening our hearts and teaching others what we have come to understand, we tend to accelerate the progress we make on our own personal journey.

Whether or not we choose to teach formally, we need to consider how to live our lives in harmony with our newfound levels of awareness. The old, conditioned habits of mind that have guided our lives in the past may no longer effectively serve us.

Are we eating mindfully, not eating more than is required to maintain good health? Are we exercising to keep the body fit, enabling us to continue making progress on our path? Are we avoiding contact with those whose minds tend to dwell on thoughts of hatred or sensual pleasures? Are we cultivating relationships with individuals who are wise—those who consistently strive to maintain equanimity and to keep thoughts of loving-kindness and compassion at the forefront of their minds? Are we engaging in forms of livelihood that avoid bringing harm to anyone either directly or indirectly? Does our work contribute to the furthering of peace, goodwill, and wisdom in the world?

The purpose of the final exercise is to help you consider the ways in which you will live your life as a teaching.

EXERCISE: LIVING LIFE AS A TEACHING

Please answer the following questions after giving them serious consideration:

1. What will you teach others about *health* through the way in which you take care of your own body?
2. What will you teach others about *relationships* through the way in which you communicate with others?
3. What will you teach others about *work* through the way in which you serve others?
4. What will you teach others about *love* through the way in which you are "present" with others?
5. What will you teach others about the path to *enlightenment* through the way in which you have been making your journey?

Please open your journal (Journal Entry 13) and record the thoughts, feelings, images, and insights that arose during this stage of your journey. You can use the following questions as a way of exploring your experience. There are no right or wrong answers.

❖ Who were the teachers that made a significant contribution to your spiritual development? Which of their attributes have most profoundly affected you?

❖ How do you know when you are teaching from your knowledge as opposed to teaching from your direct experience?

❖ If you are considering becoming a spiritual guide to others, what do you believe motivates this interest?

❖ What life transformations—in terms of your physical well-being, relationships, forms of livelihood, and clarity of mind—have you experienced from the time you began this journey?

Journal Entry 13   *Date:* _____

_____

_____

_____

_____

_____

_____

_____

_____

_____

_____

_____

_____

_____

_____

_____

_____

_____

_____

_____

_____

_____

_____

_____

_____

_____

_____

_____

_____

_____

CONCLUSION

At the onset of this book, it was stated that our work together would be intense, that the views along the way would be extraordinary, and that the overall experience would be transformative. Our intention was to move beyond externals in order to reach the very essence of our lives. We were working to come home to a place of unconditional love and inner peace.

The journey began with the recognition that what we truly seek is contentment. You discovered how this contentment comes from within and how your self-image has either helped or hindered your realization of inner peace. You dealt with issues that may have kept you emotionally tied to the past or afraid to move confidently into the future. You learned how to meditate and live in the "here and now" of your life. You may even have realized who you are beyond your self-definitions and reached the very center of your being.

As you have certainly discovered, the path is not an easy one to follow, and the goal may sometimes appear to be farther away than when we first began. Do not lose heart—your aspirations may be achieved in the very next moment.

There was once a little boy who had everything: parents who loved him, lots of toys to play with, and good food to eat. But it never seemed to be enough.

One day he read about a wishing tree. The story described the tree and said that anyone who sat under it could have anything he or she wanted. The little boy was determined to find that tree. He rode around the neighborhood on his bicycle looking for the tree, but it was nowhere to be found. When he got older, he drove his car from coast to coast looking for the tree, but to no avail. Never giving up, he dedicated his entire life to the search.

The little boy eventually grew into an old man who had wasted his youth and middle age looking for the wishing tree. One day he sat down in a park in total despair and began to cry. The wind heard his crying and out of compassion offered to carry the old man back to his home. Along the way, the wind asked the old man why he was crying such bitter tears. As the old man told the story of his life, the wind began to laugh uproariously. "Why do you mock me?" asked the old man. "I am not mocking you," replied the wind. "The wishing tree you were looking for—you were sitting under it when I found you!"

We've all been on this journey for a long time. Those who have reached the center have called out—as if with one voice—proclaiming the joys of spiritual freedom. Paradoxically, the path illuminated by the oxherding pictures leads to a place we never truly left—we have always been free, lacking only the conscious awareness of our freedom. We are sitting under that wishing tree right now. At the end of our journey, we can finally claim what has always been ours from the start.

SUGGESTED READINGS

Blofeld, John, trans. *The Zen Teaching of Huang Po*. New York: Grove Press, 1958.

Frey, Diane, and C. Jesse Carlock. *Enhancing Self-Esteem*. 2d ed. Muncie, IN: Accelerated Development, 1989.

Gunaratana, Henepola. *Mindfulness in Plain English*. Boston: Wisdom, 1993.

Jeffers, Susan. *Feel the Fear and Do It Anyway*. New York: Random House, 1988.

Kornfield, Jack. *A Path with Heart*. New York: Bantam, 1993.

Lao Tsu. *Tao Te Ching*. Translated by Gia-Fu Feng and Jane English. New York: Random House, 1972.

Levine, Stephen. *A Gradual Awakening*. New York: Doubleday, 1979.

———. *Who Dies?* New York: Doubleday, 1982.

Mahasi Sayadaw. *The Progress of Insight*. Kandy, Sri Lanka: Buddhist Publication Society, 1978.

Nyanaponika Thera. *The Heart of Buddhist Meditation*. York Beach, ME: Samuel Weiser, 1976.

Rando, Therese A. *Grief, Dying, and Death*. Champaign, IL: Research Press Company, 1984.

Reps, Paul. *Zen Flesh, Zen Bones*. New York: Doubleday, 1961.

Salzberg, Sharon. *Lovingkindness: The Revolutionary Art of Happiness*. Boston: Shambhala, 1995.

Silananda, U. *The Four Foundations of Mindfulness.* Boston: Wisdom, 1990.

Soma Thera. *The Way of Mindfulness.* 5th ed. Kandy, Sri Lanka: Buddhist Publication Society, 1967.

INDEX

living in the moment and,
157
selflessness and, 180
unskillful states and, 166
feelings. *See* emotion
finances, 25–26, 31, 36, 48, 89,
107–14
flute players, 158
forgiveness, 58, 65–75, 84
expressing, 68–75
journal-keeping and, 74–75
of one's self, 71–75
of others, 67–71
freedom, 3, 85, 160
from dualism, 180, 181
forgiveness and, 71, 74
reaching the source and,
195–97
self-definitions and, 190
from self-identification, 179
skillful states and, 174
the story of the wishing tree
and, 214
friendship, 140–41, 170. *See also*
relationships

G

generosity, 138, 166, 183
goals
attaining, 48–50
becoming aware and, 103–5
clear comprehension and,
138–45
living in the moment and,
154
self-image and, 47–50

slow progress towards,
164–65
unachieved, 31–32
unskillful states and, 166
goose-in-the-bottle story,
183–84
greed, 2, 138, 182, 207
grief. *See also* death; loss
anticipatory, 78
bypassing and, 59
confronting fear and, 98, 99
journal-keeping and, 85–88
resolving, 78–86
shadow self and, 43
three stages of, 78–79
unfinished business and,
83–84, 85, 86
unresolved, 55
guided imagery, 84–85, 89–91
guilt, 8, 22, 34, 42, 65–66, 72,
79

H

half lotus position, 9–11
happiness, 3, 119, 197
confronting fear and, 98, 100
versus inner peace, 15–16
repressed memories and, 36
skillful states and, 172–73
use of the term, 15
hatred, 2, 182, 207
clear comprehension and, 138
cost of maintaining, 67
forgiveness and, 66–67, 73
self-, 73
unskillful states and, 166

W
walking meditation, 128–35. *See also* insight meditation
wealth. *See* money
wishing tree, 213–14
wisdom, 55–56, 138, 183, 209

workplace, 21, 107–14. *See also* careers
world, integrating new understanding in the, 5, 205–14
writing. *See* journal-keeping

ABOUT THE AUTHOR

MATTHEW FLICKSTEIN has been an insight meditation teacher for over thirty years. A psychotherapist for most of his professional career, Matthew has created many personal development workshops and has trained thousands of people. He has also certified other psychotherapists to lead stress management and personal development workshops that he created.

Matthew earned his B.S. degree from the University of Maryland, an M.S. degree in counseling and psychotherapy from Loyola College, and completed Ph.D. coursework at the Saybrook Institute. He interned at Johns Hopkins Counseling and Psychiatric Center in Baltimore.

In 1984 Matthew co-founded the Bhavana Society, a Buddhist monastic center in West Virginia, with Venerable Henepola Gunaratana. He was subsequently ordained and lived at the center as a Theravadan Buddhist monk. Matthew is also the founder of the Forest Way Insight Meditation Center.

In addition to *The Meditator's Workbook*, Matthew has published *The Meditator's Atlas* and edited the best-selling meditation manual *Mindfulness in Plain English* by Bhante Gunaratana. He is currently producing a spiritual documentary entitled *With One Voice*.

ABOUT WISDOM PUBLICATIONS

WISDOM PUBLICATIONS, a nonprofit publisher, is dedicated to making available authentic works relating to Buddhism for the benefit of all. We publish books by ancient and modern masters in all traditions of Buddhism, translations of important texts, and original scholarship. Additionally, we offer books that explore East-West themes unfolding as traditional Buddhism encounters our modern culture in all its aspects. Our titles are published with the appreciation of Buddhism as a living philosophy, and with the special commitment to preserve and transmit important works from Buddhism's many traditions.

To learn more about Wisdom, or to browse books online, visit our website at www.wisdompubs.org.

You may request a copy of our catalog online or by writing to this address:

Wisdom Publications
199 Elm Street
Somerville, Massachusetts 02144 USA
Telephone: 617-776-7416
Fax: 617-776-7841
Email: info@wisdompubs.org
www.wisdompubs.org

THE WISDOM TRUST

As a nonprofit publisher, Wisdom is dedicated to the publication of Dharma books for the benefit of all sentient beings and dependent upon the kindness and generosity of sponsors in order to do so. If you would like to make a donation to Wisdom, you may do so through our website or our Somerville office. If you would like to help sponsor the publication of a book, please write or email us at the address above.

Thank you.

Wisdom is a nonprofit, charitable 501(c)(3) organization affiliated with the Foundation for the Preservation of the Mahayana Tradition (FPMT).

Also Available from Wisdom Publications

The Meditator's Atlas
A Roadmap to the Inner World
Matthew Flickstein | foreword by Bhante Henepola Gunaratana
208 pages | 0-86171-337-0 | $15.95

"A monumental synthesis from the standpoint of one who has walked the path. A simple fact shouts from these pages over and over again—that nirvana is possible."—*Inquiring Mind*

Mindfulness in Plain English
Bhante Henepola Gunaratana
224 pages | 0-86171-321-4 | $14.95

"A masterpiece. I cannot recommend it highly enough."—Jon Kabat-Zinn

Beyond Mindfulness in Plain English
Bhante Henepola Gunaratana
200 pages | 0-86171-529-2 | $15.95

In his characteristically warm, clear, and friendly voice, Bhante introduces us to the "jhanas"—deeply calm, joyous, and powerful states of meditation that, when explored with the clearly presented tools Bhante Gunaratana gives us, a lead to life of insight and unshakeable peace.

Real Meditation in Minutes a Day
Enhancing Your Performance, Relationships, Spirituality, and Health
Joseph Arpaia and Lobsang Rapgay
264 pages | 0-86171-556-X | $16.95

"Like a test-prep for life.'"—*Newsweek.*